M000187469

ESSENTIALS
of Technical
Analysis for
Financial Markets

ESSENTIALS SERIES

The Essentials Series was created for busy business advisory and corporate professionals. The books in this series were designed so that these busy professionals can quickly acquire knowledge and skills in core business areas.

Each book provides need-to-have fundamentals for those professionals who must:

- Get up to speed quickly, because they have been promoted to a new position or have broadened their responsibility scope
- Manage a new functional area
- Brush up on new developments in their area of responsibility
- Add more value to their company or clients

Other books in this series include:

Essentials of Accounts Payable, Mary S. Schaeffer

Essentials of Balanced Scorecard, Mohan Nair

Essentials of Business Ethics, Denis Collins

Essentials of Business Process Outsourcing, Thomas N. Duening and Rick L. Click

Essentials of Capacity Management, Reginald Tomas Yu-Lee

Essentials of Cash Flow, H.A. Schaeffer, Jr.

Essentials of Corporate Fraud, Tracy L. Coenen

Essentials of Corporate Governance, Sanjay Anand

Essentials of Corporate Performance Measurement, George T. Friedlob, Lydia L.F. Schleifer, and Franklin J. Plewa, Jr.

Essentials of Cost Management, Joe and Catherine Stenzel

Essentials of Credit, Collections, and Accounts Receivable, Mary S. Schaeffer

Essentials of CRM: A Guide to Customer Relationship Management, Bryan Bergeron

Essentials of Enterprise Compliance, Susan D. Conway and Mara E. Conway

Essentials of Financial Analysis, George T. Friedlob and Lydia L. F. Schleifer

Essentials of Financial Risk Management, Karen A. Horcher

Essentials of Foreign Exchange Trading, James Chen

Essentials of Licensing Intellectual Property, Paul J. Lerner and Alexander I. Poltorak

Essentials of Knowledge Management, Bryan Bergeron

Essentials of Managing Corporate Cash, Michele Allman-Ward and James Sagner

Essentials of Managing Treasury, Karen A. Horcher

Essentials of Patents, Andy Gibbs and Bob DeMatteis

Essentials of Payroll Management and Accounting, Steven M. Bragg

Essentials of Sarbanes-Oxley, Sanjay Anand

Essentials of Shared Services, Bryan Bergeron

Essentials of Supply Chain Management, Michael Hugos

Essentials of Trademarks and Unfair Competition, Dana Shilling

Essentials of XBRL, Bryan Bergeron

For more information on any of the above titles, please visit www.wiley.com.

ESSENTIALS

of Technical Analysis for Financial Markets

James Chen

WILEY

John Wiley & Sons, Inc.

Published by John Wiley & Sons, Inc., Hoboken, New Jersey.
Published simultaneously in Canada.

For general information on our other products and services or for technical support, please contact our Customer Care Department within the United States at (800) 762-2974, outside the United States at (317) 572-3993 or fax (317) 572-4002.

Wiley publishes in a variety of print and electronic formats and by print-on-demand. Some material included with standard print versions of this book may not be included in e-books or in print-on-demand. If this book refers to media such as a CD or DVD that is not included in the version you purchased, you may download this material at http://booksupport.wiley.com. For more information about Wiley products, visit www.wiley.com.

Library of Congress Cataloging-in-Publication Data:
Chen, James, 1971-
  Essentials of technical analysis for financial markets / James Chen.
    p. cm.—(Essentials series)
  Includes index.
  ISBN 978-0-470-53729-9 (pbk.)
1. Investment analysis.   I. Title.
  HG4529.C456 2010
  332.63'2042—dc22   2009051054

ISBN-13 978-0-470-53729-9

10 9 8 7 6 5 4 3 2 1

*To my parents, my wife,
my children, and technical
analysts everywhere*

Contents

Preface   xiii

Acknowledgments   xvii

1 Introduction to Technical Analysis:

Pursuing Profit in the Financial Markets   **1**

What Is Technical Analysis?   2

Technical versus Fundamental   2

Methods   5

What to Expect   5

Summary   9

2 The Story of Technical Analysis:

From the Japanese Rice Markets to

Dow Theory to Automated Trading   **11**

The Beginning: Japanese Rice Markets   12

Dow Theory   14

Charting   17

Elliott Wave   18

W. D. Gann   20

Indicators   20

Contents

Trend Followers   22

Market Technicians Association   23

Technical Analysis Today   23

Summary   24

3   The Power of Technical Analysis:

Principles of Price Action   27

Introduction to Price Action Concepts   28

Components of Price Action   29

Summary   32

4   The Basics of Technical Analysis:

Bars, Candlesticks, Lines,

and Point and Figure   33

Bars and Candlesticks   34

Line Charts   37

Point-and-Figure Charts   38

Summary   40

5   The Heart of Technical Analysis:

Uptrends and Downtrends   41

Introduction to Trend   42

Effect of Time Frames on Trend Determination   50

Parallel Trend Channels   52

Trend Lines   54

Summary   55

6   The Soul of Technical Analysis:

Support and Resistance   57

Introduction to Support and Resistance   58

Contents

Support Becomes Resistance Becomes Support   60

Summary   64

7   Primary Drawing Tools: Trend Lines, Trend Channels, and Horizontal Support and Resistance   **65**

Introduction to Drawing Tools   66

Static Support and Resistance   67

Dynamic Support and Resistance   72

Horizontal Support and Resistance Lines   78

Trend Lines   81

Parallel Trend Channels   87

Summary   89

8   Chart Patterns: Bar Shapes and Candlestick Formations   **91**

Introduction to Chart Patterns   91

Continuation Bar Patterns   93

Reversal Bar Patterns   102

Gaps   106

Candlestick Patterns   110

Single-Candle Patterns   111

Multiple-Candle Patterns   116

Summary   118

9   The World of Moving Averages   **119**

Introduction to Moving Averages   119

Moving Average Crossovers   123

Moving Averages as Support and Resistance   131

Summary   134

Contents

10   Key Technical Indicators and Oscillators   **135**

Introduction to Indicators and Oscillators   135

Key Indicators   139

Key Oscillators   148

Summary   159

11   Fibonacci and Elliott Wave   **161**

Fibonacci Theory and Methods   161

Elliott Wave Theory   170

Summary   175

12   Point-and-Figure Charting   **177**

Introduction to Point and Figure   177

Point-and-Figure Patterns   181

Point-and-Figure Price Targets   188

Summary   190

13   Volume   **193**

Introduction to Volume   193

On-Balance Volume   196

Tick Volume   198

Summary   199

**14   Technical Trading Strategies: Practical
Applications**   **201**

Introduction to Technical Trading Strategies   202

Moving Average Crossovers   203

Breakout Trading   212

Trend Trading   224

Contents

Range Trading   238

Price-Oscillator Divergences   244

Oscillator Trading   249

Fibonacci Trading   254

Positive Expectancy   256

Summary   258

15 Risk Control and Money Management   261

Introduction to Risk Control and

Money Management   262

Stop-Losses   263

Reward:Risk Ratio   266

Maximum Allowable Loss   269

Multiple Fractional Positions   271

Diversification   273

Summary   273

Index   277

Preface

The practice of technical analysis has grown at a remarkably rapid pace in the last few decades. Traders, investors, and analysts involved in all of the various financial markets have increasingly turned to the principles of technical analysis both to interpret as well as to act on market price behavior. These practitioners recognize that technical analysis provides a concrete, logical, and effective approach to tackling any major financial market.

In addition, the development of new methods and techniques within the realm of technical analysis has been equally rapid. Whether it is the latest and greatest technical indicator or a fresh and innovative way to denote support and resistance, technical analysis has generally progressed in a swift, continuous manner since its inception. Many of these new developments have contributed substantially to the further evolution of the field.

Consequently, innumerable specialties and subspecialties have developed within the discipline of technical analysis. In my years as an analyst and trader, however, I have deliberately refrained from having my primary focus "progress" onto excessively complex or esoteric concepts within the field. As a result, many have asked me why I keep my analysis and trading so simple. My answer is always the same: Simple, at least in the arenas of technical analysis and technical trading, works quite well. Therefore, I have consistently preferred to focus all concentration on the essentials, as opposed to diluting attention on the countless areas of technical analysis that can possibly be focused on.

A quick look at any one of my daily or intraday analysis charts will illustrate my general approach. I like to draw lines, and lots of them—short lines, long lines, horizontal lines, angled lines, line shapes, and everything in between. I tend to keep the mechanical indicators on my charts to a minimum, although anything that helps me better identify the trend (like moving averages) and the key support/resistance levels within a given market is a welcomed element in my trading arsenal.

In light of the simplicity of this approach, if I was asked to summarize the essence of technical analysis and technical trading in a concise, working description, it would probably be this: the study of how mass market behavior affects the manner in which market prices move in relation to the trend and support/resistance.

When all of the layers are peeled away, these are essentially the elements that remain. In fact, the majority of mainstream technical analysis tools and studies ultimately just help define or act on the trend, support/resistance, or a combination of both.

To clarify further, the concept of trend can refer to a directional price move, a reversal of the prior directional price move, or a lack of direction in the market altogether. The concept of support/resistance can refer to static price levels (unchanging levels at which a market may react in a significant manner) or to dynamically changing price levels (as in an ascending or descending trend line).

Staying on the theme of keeping it simple, although different technical analysts gravitate toward different techniques and methods, I would strongly stress the fact that the most successful practitioners tend to concentrate primarily on only one or a few aspects of the discipline. If one is able to know a particular method inside and out—whether it is drawing trend lines, using the relative strength index, counting Elliott Waves, trading Fibonacci retracements, identifying reversal patterns, or any one of the countless other technical approaches to the financial markets—the path to trading success will likely be much smoother than if one attempts to dabble in a little bit of everything. Again, keeping it simple by mastering one or a few essential aspects of technical analysis is much preferred over diluting attention in all different directions.

With that having been said, this book should act as your straightforward guide to the wealth of essential methods and approaches that are available within the field of financial technical analysis. There is much to choose from within these pages, but once a focus is established, the rest is simply a matter of exhaustive further study, experimentation, and experience.

Good luck and good trading.

James Chen

Acknowledgments

For their tremendous support and understanding during the time I was writing this book, as well as in all other aspects of life, I would like to thank my parents, Shou Lien and Hsiao-wen; my brother and sister, Jack and Julie; my wife, Dongping; my sons, Tommy and Kevin; and my newborn daughter, Emily.

Additionally, I would like to acknowledge all of the tireless hard work and support from the wonderful editors at John Wiley & Sons, including Tim Burgard and Stacey Rivera, who also published my previous book, *Essentials of Foreign Exchange Trading* (2009).

Sincere gratitude also goes out to these trading industry luminaries for generously contributing their knowledge and expertise in the form of insightful book passages: Robert Prechter, Jr.; Steve Nison; Alexander Elder; and Michael Covel.

Finally, I would like to give a big thanks to my many colleagues at FX Solutions who have consistently shown a great deal of interest and encouragement during the course of my writing this book.

CHAPTER 1

Introduction to Technical Analysis

Pursuing Profit in the Financial Markets

After reading this chapter, you will be able to:

- Understand the general concept of technical analysis.
- Discern the basic differences between technical analysis and fundamental analysis.
- Recognize some of the key tools and methods of technical analysis.
- Know what concepts will be discussed throughout the rest of this book.

What Is Technical Analysis?

Technical analysis is the study of how past and present price action in a given financial market may help determine its future direction. At the same time, however, technical analysis should not be considered a crystal ball. Rather, the skills of a technical analyst are used primarily to help determine the highest-probability reactions to past and current price movement, as well as likely future price movement. Therefore, technical analysis is less about actually predicting the future and more about finding high-probability potential opportunities to trade in the financial markets.

The primary tool used by technical analysts is the ubiquitous price chart, which generally plots prices over a given period of time. The various major chart types are discussed in detail in Chapter 4, which covers the basics of technical analysis. Different analysts/ traders may choose to use different types of charts at different times, whether it is a line chart, a bar chart, a candlestick chart, a point-and-figure chart, or any of a number of other chart types.

Technical versus Fundamental

When many people in the financial world refer to technical analysis, it is often in direct contrast to the other major school of market analysis, fundamental analysis. The contrast between the two is clear and distinct.

Fundamental analysis focuses on what the underlying reasons may be for market movement. In the stock market, this would consist of news and financial information (e.g., earnings) that are directly associated with a particular publicly traded company. In the futures market, it would consist of substantive market information regarding a specific commodity (e.g., wheat or oil) or financial market/index (e.g., S&P 500). In the foreign exchange, or currency, market, fundamental analysis would be primarily concerned with international economies, central bank policy, interest rates, and inflation.

Fundamental analysis stands in stark contrast to the world of technical analysis. Instead of concerning itself with the underlying reasons for price movement, technical analysis focuses on the price movement itself and how mass human behavior is manifested in price action. Technical analysts believe that all fundamental information and economic factors that can cause price movement are already reflected in price action. Therefore, technical analysis purists generally avoid looking at earnings or crop reports or international economic conditions. Instead, the two primary tools of price and volume as depicted on a financial chart are sufficient for most analysts of the technical persuasion. Of these two tools, price is universally more important.

Here is another way to describe the distinction between fundamental analysis and technical analysis: While fundamental analysis may concern itself with the myriad reasons "why" price moves, technical analysis is single-mindedly focused on "how" price moves and the way in which that might affect future price movement. Technical analysis consists of a broad methodology through which traders can identify trading opportunities and make all of their most important trading decisions. This includes trade entries, trade exits, stop-loss placement, profit target placement, trade sizing, risk management, and more.

While some traders and investors are strict adherents to either fundamental analysis or technical analysis, and completely exclude consideration of the other, many use a combination of both.

EXECUTIVE INSIGHT

Robert Prechter, Jr., CMT

In a written interview with the author, Robert Prechter, Jr., publisher of *The Elliott Wave Theorist* since 1979 and founder/president of Elliott Wave International (elliottwave.com), discusses being a pure technician. Legendary for his market timing and trading acumen utilizing Elliott Wave principles, Prechter has won numerous major accolades from the media and financial community over an illustrious, decades-long career. He has authored many books, several of which were instrumental in bringing Ralph Nelson Elliott's groundbreaking Elliott Wave Principle into the forefront of financial market analysis. More about Robert Prechter, Jr., and his considerable contributions to the development of technical analysis can be found in Chapter 2.

Prechter states:

> Most analysts are not technicians. But it is also true that most self-described technicians are not pure technicians. They talk about Federal Reserve policy, political action, economic news and other such events as causal to the market's movement. If such events are causal, then technical indicators would not be potent, because randomly occurring outside events would be creating the supposed patterns, making them spurious. Any new event could make the market go contrary to what a pattern or indicator suggested. To be a hybrid analyst is to be theoretically inconsistent. Either outside events move the market or market behavior is patterned. One cannot have it both ways.

> A pure technician is someone who believes that the stock market's causality derives from unchanging aspects of human behavior. Only if this is true can a head-and-shoulders pattern, a trend line, or a wave form be reliable. Otherwise such things are simply artifacts of random movement. True technicians are those who rely solely on technical indicators and models such as price trends, cycles, volume patterns, momentum readings, sentiment indicators, Elliott Waves, Edwards and Magee patterns, and Dow theory.

Fundamentalists look for outside causes and try to predict
them, reasoning from those predictions to market predictions.
Technicians study patterns relating to market behavior and
make decisions on that basis alone. Fundamentalists study
everything but the behavior of the market. Technicians study
only the behavior of the market.

Methods

The methods of utilizing technical analysis are many and varied.
They include such ubiquitous concepts as head and shoulders, support and resistance, trends, moving averages, and double-tops. But
they also include concepts that are less popularly known, such as
linear regression, bullish engulfing patterns, Elliott Wave, and point-
and-figure charts. All of these elements of technical analysis, and
much more, are discussed in the pages of this book.

The main focus of this book is to provide the essential knowledge
about technical analysis that is necessary to begin serious analysis of
any major financial market. With that goal, this book outlines and
describes the primary tools used by technical analysts and traders.
Of course, technical analysis is a huge subject that is growing every
day, and no book could ever hope to cover all of the information
within the field adequately. Therefore, this book provides substantial
coverage of the essentials, as the title suggests, while necessarily omit-
ting some of the more esoteric concepts in the field.

What to Expect

After this introduction, Chapter 2 begins with a concise history of
the most pivotal events in the development of technical analysis—

from the Japanese rice markets in Osaka; to the revolutionary tenets of Dow theory; to the development and mainstream adoption of charting; to the advent of Elliott Wave theory; to the emergence of trend following; and finally to the automated, systematic trading of today.

Then the most important aspect of technical analysis, price action, is described in detail in Chapter 3. Price action, or the patterned behavior of price that can give clues as to potential future direction, is truly the basis for the study of technical analysis as we know it today.

The book then jumps straight into the primary basics of technical analysis—charts. These are the primary tools of technical analysts and traders, whether the chart of choice is a line chart, a bar chart, a candlestick chart, a point-and-figure chart, or some other manner of graphically depicting price action. All of these chart types are presented and discussed in Chapter 4, including their structures and methods of interpretation.

After these basics are covered, Chapter 5 is devoted entirely to what is arguably the single most important concept within technical analysis and the heart of the discipline: trend. The definitions and characteristics of uptrends, downtrends, and no trend are covered, as well as methods to identify trend conditions.

After the heart of technical analysis is discussed, Chapter 6 talks about another vital aspect of the field that can be considered the soul of technical analysis: support and resistance. These twin concepts are the basis for much of the technical analysis that is published in the media as well as for many technical trading methods and strategies.

The chapter on support and resistance is followed by a discussion of the practical drawing tools necessary for depicting both trends and support/resistance levels. These important drawing tools include trend lines, trend channels, and horizontal support and resistance lines. Chapter 7 covers how these lines are customarily drawn and interpreted by technical analysts and traders.

Moving on to Chapter 8, the discussion then turns to the key topic of chart patterns. This includes the most prevalent and important bar chart shapes, such as triangles, wedges, flags, pennants, head and shoulders, and the like. The chapter also includes descriptions of the most common Japanese candlestick formations, such as hammers, shooting stars, doji, engulfing patterns, and the like.

Chapter 9 covers the world of moving averages, those wavy lines that can reveal so much about a market's trending conditions and support/resistance areas. Moving averages also play a pivotal role in many technical trading strategies, as well as in market analysts' commentaries.

Besides moving averages, many other important technical indicators are mathematically derived from price. The most common and important of these indicators, which include a special subcategory called oscillators, are presented and described in Chapter 10.

From there, this book moves into the more advanced concepts of Fibonacci and Elliott Wave theories in Chapter 11. These unique perspectives on market price action are often used by more sophisticated technical traders, and they can provide extremely valuable insight into the structure of price and how to reap potential benefit from it.

Chapter 12 covers yet another unique perspective on price action: point-and-figure charting. Significantly different from its line, bar, and candlestick cousins, point-and-figure analysis concentrates exclusively on the market's price action, excluding all other factors, including time and volume. Because of this fact, many consider point-and-figure trading to be the purest form of price action trading.

Although volume is customarily excluded on point and figure charts, it is the star of Chapter 13. Used primarily by stock market traders, volume is considered both a leading indicator as well as a confirming indicator. When trading equities, volume can be a vital tool for providing important confirmation of price action. Confirmation is a key concept within technical analysis.

Chapter 14 brings together all of the tools, methods, and concepts of technical analysis discussed up to that point and describes specific trading methods and strategies used by professional technical traders. This discussion includes information on both manual and automated trading and on how each strategy covered is suited to either mode of trading. The strategies and methods described in Chapter 14 comprise the culmination of all the building blocks of information found throughout the rest of the book.

Finally, Chapter 15 discusses one of the most important aspects of any trading plan: risk control and money management. Although it is not nearly as enthusiastically embraced a topic as trade entry strategies, at least with many novice traders, most successful and professional traders/investors would likely agree that risk control and money management are the keys to consistent success in the financial markets. Without these vital components of a sound trading plan, failure can almost be assured. Chapter 15 covers some of the most important aspects of a good risk and money management plan.

By the end of this book, the goal is for the reader to be well on his or her way to becoming well rounded and knowledgeable on the art and science of technical analysis. To truly master any of the concepts discussed in this book will require further study and a lot of practical, hands-on experience. But once that mastery occurs, one invariably finds that it is always well worth the effort to get there. This book is meant to serve as an essential guide pointing the way to eventual mastery of technical analysis concepts and applications.

Summary

This chapter delved into the basic concepts of technical analysis, including a core definition and the differences between technical analysis and the other main school of financial market study, fundamental analysis.

The sharp contrast between technical analysis and fundamental analysis is useful in helping those who are new to the financial markets understand how each discipline may fit into one's overall market outlook. Fundamental analysis is more concerned with "why" price may move, while technical analysis focuses on "how" price moves. Technical analysis helps traders and investors to identify trading opportunities, which include trade entries, exits, risk management, and more.

This introductory chapter then went on to describe what is covered in each subsequent chapter. All of the essentials of technical analysis for financial markets are covered in these chapters.

CHAPTER 2

The Story of Technical Analysis

From the Japanese Rice Markets to Dow Theory to Automated Trading

 After reading this chapter, you will be able to:

- Appreciate the key developments within the history of technical analysis.
- Identify some of the most important historical contributors to the technical analysis body of knowledge.
- Understand some of the most vital components of Dow theory.

The Beginning: Japanese Rice Markets

Technical analysis has had a long and colorful history marked by the emergence of many different characters who have had a significant combined influence on the course of the major financial markets.

From what is known about the earliest use of technical analysis, traders in the Japanese rice markets of the early eighteenth century employed technical methods in their trading that were developed by a rice merchant named Honma Munehisa. These methods were eventually to become what we know today as candlestick chart trading. Much later, these techniques were introduced to the Western financial world by a pioneering trader and technical analyst named Steve Nison.

 **EXECUTIVE INSIGHT**

Steve Nison, CMT

In a written interview with the author, Steve Nison, who is currently president of CandleCharts.com and author of the definitive book on the subject of candlesticks, *Japanese Candlestick Charting Techniques*, discusses "why technical analysis."
Nison states:

> I frequently give on-site and Web-based custom seminars to some of the top financial firms. Interestingly, some of these, up until they "saw the light" with Nison candlesticks, had used only fundamental analysis. Since this book focuses on technical analysis, I want to relate to those of you new to this field what I related to these institutional clients about the importance of technical analysis:
>
> **1.** Technical analysis incorporates all information, whether known by insiders or the general public.

2. There are two factors that influence price—our rational side (what fundamentals gauge like p/e [price/earnings] ratios) and our emotional side ("I have to get out NOW!"). And the only way to gauge the emotional component of the market is through charts.

3. As the Japanese proverb states, "Like the right hand helping the left," so it is with technical and fundamental analysis. Both of these help round the circle of analysis. Companies I have worked with may have 10 stocks on their fundamental buy list. So they would use technical analysis and our candlestick insights to determine which are technically best to buy. After all, would it make sense to buy a stock that is under support? So fundamentals, in this case, give them what to buy. And technicals help with the timing.

4. Technical analysis helps foster a risk and money management approach to the market. This is because the most powerful aspect of charts is that there is always a price that says we are wrong. By the time the fundamentals change, it may be too late.

5. By unemotionally analyzing a chart, it helps foster an objective view of the market. So if the market is rallying and making higher closes, but if each of these sessions are shooting stars or candle lines with longer upper shadows, it is a warning that the market is, as the Japanese would say, "rising in agony." This means, in spite of the higher closes, if you looked at the market objectively with these bearish upper shadows on the chart, it should be a cause for concern.

6. Since so many traders and analysts use technical analysis, it often has a major impact on the market. As such, it is important to be alerted to technical signals others may be using.

In the rice markets of Osaka during the early eighteenth century, Honma Munehisa found great trading success using techniques based on the psychology of the market. This was an almost revolutionary way of viewing financial markets at the time. Besides authoring several books on the principles that were later to fall under the umbrella of candlestick analysis, Honma eventually became one of the most profitable financial traders in history.

Dow Theory

Fast-forward to the late nineteenth century in America. Charles Dow (born 1851) is considered the father of technical analysis in the West. He originated a theory, later named Dow theory, which outlined his views on price action in the stock market. Dow was one of the founders of Dow Jones and Company as well as the first editor of the *Wall Street Journal*. After Charles Dow's death in 1902, Dow theory was further refined by others, primarily William Hamilton, Robert Rhea, E. George Shaefer, and Richard Russell.

Although there is significant controversy in modern times regarding the original concepts behind Dow theory, this group of principles forms the general underlying basis for Western technical analysis as practiced today by millions of market participants.

It should be kept in mind when evaluating Dow theory that the principles were originally based primarily on two stock market average indexes: industrial (manufacturing) and rail (now transportation). In the present day, however, concepts of Dow theory can be applied to all market indexes and can be extended to all major financial markets. According to Dow theory, there are several primary principles of market price action. They can be summarized in this way.

- **The market discounts everything.** All news and fundamental market information is always priced into the market or reflected in market prices. Since these market prices are based on human knowledge and expectations, they are constantly adjusting to accommodate and reflect all relevant information, including all actual news as well as any potential future events that may be expected, feared, or hoped for. In other words, all events and speculation on events are always already reflected in the current market price.

- **Three trends.** Financial markets (or, according to Dow, the stock market average indexes) are comprised of three trends: primary, secondary, and minor. A primary trend is a major directional price move, whether up or down, that usually lasts between one and three years. A secondary trend can be characterized as a medium-term swing, often a countertrend reaction, which usually retraces between one-third and two-thirds of the primary trend and lasts from around three weeks to three months. Finally, a minor trend is a short-term price move that can last anywhere from a few hours to several weeks. Minor trends exist within the context of secondary trends, which in turn are often reactions to primary trends.

- **Three phases.** According to Dow theory, the most important trend, by far, is the primary trend. There are generally three phases within a primary trend. In an uptrend, these three phases are accumulation, public participation, and then excess. Accumulation in a new uptrend occurs at the tail end of a downtrend, when the smart investors are beginning to buy once again. The public participation phase, which is usually the longest phase, then commences when the investing public begins to recognize the new uptrend and to enter into it. Finally, the excess phase begins when the smart investors start to sell off their positions to late market entrants that are getting in at exactly the wrong time. At the tail end of the excess phase, signs begin to point to a possible start of a new, opposite primary trend, in this case a downtrend. Similar to uptrends, downtrends also have three phases: distribution, public participation, and excess.

- **Confirmation.** This concept was originally meant to apply to two stock market average indexes: industrial (or manufacturing stocks) and rail (now transportation stocks). Dow asserted that these two indexes have to confirm each other by moving in the same direction before a trend determination can be made. In other words, a stock market uptrend is an uptrend only if the two indexes are both in clear uptrends. In the present day, confirmation within the field of technical analysis has gone in a completely different direction, but it remains as vitally important today as it was in Dow's time.

- **Volume confirms trends.** Although price is always of utmost importance, volume is used as an important confirmation of price action. Price movement in the direction of the trend should be accompanied by high volume, while countertrend corrections should be accompanied by significantly decreased volume. If volume confirms the trend in this manner, it is an indication that the trend is strong and should continue.

- **Trends are valid until reversed.** Trends continue until there is clear evidence that a bona fide reversal has occurred. This means that while countertrend corrections and consolidative price action may occur, only a clear reversal indication can signal the end of a trend. While one of the goals of technical analysis is to differentiate clear reversals from corrective price action within a continuing trend, this is one of the key challenges for any trader or investor.

While much has changed since Dow's time, the core principles of Dow theory continue to provide a foundational basis for modern technical analysis. Although it would be difficult to adhere closely to Dow theory in today's trading environment, the practical tools and techniques that stem from Charles Dow's original ideas comprise a powerful approach to trading present-day financial markets.

Charting

Perhaps the most important development in the history of technical analysis was the genesis of modern-day price charts. These graphic representations of price action are the primary tools for countless technical analysts, traders, and investors involved in all of the financial markets.

As discussed in Chapter 4, there are several different types of charts available for analyzing market prices. First to develop in the United States was the point-and-figure chart, which began to come into use in the late nineteenth century, around the time that Charles Dow originated his market theories. From crude, handwritten records of market prices, point-and-figure charts gradually evolved over the years in the early twentieth century into the form that we see today, with columns of Xs for uptrends and Os for downtrends.

Also in the early twentieth century, the currently ubiquitous bar chart first came into use. Over decades of widespread adoption of this charting method, bar charts eventually became the most widely used charts in all financial markets.

The dominance of bar charts continued unchallenged until candlestick charting was formally introduced to the Western world in the late 1980s. Brought over from Japan by Steve Nison, an American technical analyst and trader, candlesticks quickly flourished to pose a serious challenge to the long-held dominance of bar charts. Although the origins of candlesticks were rooted centuries earlier in the rice markets of Japan, as mentioned previously, it was not until they had been introduced to the United States that they began to gain widespread international popularity.

From their early origins, point-and-figure charts, bar charts, and candlestick charts have all withstood the test of time and have flourished in their own ways, with different analysts and traders, and in all financial markets.

Elliott Wave

Many important industry figures after Charles Dow have contributed a great deal to the field of modern technical analysis. One of these key innovators is the originator of one of the best-known and most widely adopted models in the field of technical analysis, Elliott Wave. His name was Ralph Nelson Elliott.

Elliott was born in 1871, but he developed his elaborate theory of financial market trends in the 1930s, when he was over 60 years of age. This was after an earlier career in accounting. Elliott Wave theory is described in more detail in Chapter 11, on Fibonacci and Elliott Wave. But it should suffice to say here that Elliott's contributions to the history and practices of technical analysis have been tremendous. With his famous wave theory of stock market trends, Elliott was able to provide a concrete description of the nature of financial markets. Like Dow theory, Elliott Wave theory gave analysts, investors, and traders a market structure to work from, complete with specific rules and guidelines.

After Elliott's death in 1948, other technical analysts were able to carry on his work and perpetuate his theory with substantial success. These analysts included Charles Collins, Hamilton Bolton, and A. J. Frost. But perhaps no other individual has brought more widespread and mainstream attention to Elliott's original work than Robert Prechter, Jr., publisher of *The Elliott Wave Theorist*, founder/president of Elliott Wave International, and author of numerous bestselling financial books. Prechter single-handedly revived widespread investor interest in Elliott Wave theory through his newsletter, books, and, most important, the highly publicized accuracy of his market forecasts starting in the 1980s. One of the most prolific writers and educators on the subject of mass market psychology in the modern-day financial world, Prechter's contributions to the field of technical analysis have been, and continue to be, profound.

Besides his groundbreaking work with Elliott Wave, Prechter was also former president of the Market Technician's Association (MTA), an organization of technical analysts that has had a tremendous impact on the growth and perpetuation of technical analysis globally. Counting among its members most of the top modern-day pioneers in the field, the MTA has been a key component of the history of technical analysis since the organization's founding in the early 1970s.

W. D. Gann

William Delbert Gann, born in 1878, was a contemporary of Ralph Nelson Elliott, and his theories have also had a significant influence on the field of technical analysis, though not as strong as Elliott's. Gann was a trader who was noted both for his success in trading stocks and commodities as well as for his record in forecasting significant events, mostly reversals, in the stock market.

Gann's techniques and strategies revolved primarily around his theories on time and price, angles, and geometric proportions. This included substantial work on market cycles. His discovery in the early twentieth century of the market time factor led Gann to publicize a test of his trading skills. This live test led to phenomenal returns in a short period of time, and his fame grew exponentially as a result.

Having written several books on various topics throughout his life, Gann was a true pioneer for contributing a substantial amount of early knowledge to the field of technical analysis, much like Ralph Nelson Elliott. Today, many traders and analysts still make use of the various tools and principles inherited from the Gann legacy.

Indicators

Throughout the modern history of technical analysis, several books and publications have come to the forefront to propel the discipline to new heights. Perhaps no other single book has made as much of a historical impact as *Technical Analysis of Stock Trends* by Robert Edwards and John Magee, originally published in the late 1940s.

This book quickly became a classic, serving as the standard text in the field, and continues to command a substantial presence on traders' bookshelves around the world.

Many other books and publications that have been published since Edwards and Magee's pivotal work have been instrumental in introducing technical indicators to the mainstream public. Such staple indicators and oscillators as relative strength index (RSI), average directional index (ADX), average true range (ATR), and parabolic stop and reverse (SAR), among others, were all introduced by trader and technical analyst J. Welles Wilder. These indicators were all described in the late 1970s in his important book entitled *New Concepts in Technical Trading Systems*.

Also in the late 1970s, the popular moving average convergence/divergence (MACD) indicator was developed. MACD was developed by the technical analyst Gerald Appel. Since its introduction in the late 1970s by Appel, MACD has gone on to become one of the most widely used indicators available.

No discussion of indicators or momentum oscillators would be complete without mention of the stochastics oscillator. This widely adopted indicator can be found on the charts of many technical traders. Developed in the 1950s by the broker, trader, and analyst George Lane, stochastics is a core momentum oscillator that many traders now consider indispensable.

The commodity channel index (CCI) oscillator was first introduced by Donald Lambert in 1980. Originally designed for use in the commodities markets, as its name suggests, CCI eventually made its mark in all of the other financial markets as well.

In the early 1980s, John Bollinger, a well-known analyst and portfolio manager, developed and introduced his namesake Bollinger Bands, volatility bands that have become a standard component on the vast majority of charting platforms.

Trend Followers

Throughout the modern history of the financial markets, there have emerged many prominent traders who have used technical analysis exclusively in their trading, to substantial success. Notable among these technical traders are those who consider themselves trend followers. Among the early pioneers of this influential trading methodology was a futures trader by the name of Richard Donchian.

Donchian managed futures funds and developed a systematic approach to trading futures that capitalized on the trending nature of financial markets. The tendency of markets to move in one general direction, whether up or down, for prolonged periods was the basis for the trading style originated by Donchian.

Donchian's influence launched the trading careers of many prominent traders as well as a plethora of institutions that employ the trend-following approach. Among the most notable of these traders is a well-known group trained by another trend-following pioneer by the name of Richard Dennis. The group was informally known as the Turtles, and Dennis trained them in the 1980s to trade futures and other financial instruments using a specific trend-following methodology. Some of the Turtles went on to experience substantial success in trading and managing accounts as a result of their training in trend-following techniques.

Market Technicians Association

Beside the many traders and analysts that have influenced the course of technical analysis history, one organization, in particular, has had a large and lasting influence on the development of the field. The Market Technicians Association (MTA), as mentioned previously, is a global organization of technical analysts that has had a profound impact on standardizing technical analysis practices as well as perpetuating the use and growth of technical analysis across all financial markets. Begun in the early 1970s by a small group of dedicated pioneers in the field, the MTA has gone on to define the practice of technical analysis as we know it today. Therefore, this organization has earned a key place within the history of the field.

One of the most significant achievements of the MTA has been the development of the Chartered Market Technician (CMT) professional designation, which began in the late 1980s. The MTA provides rigorous testing of individuals on technical analysis concepts and practices and then issues the CMT designation to those who pass the series of tests. This has helped tremendously in standardizing knowledge for technical analysts as well as providing a benchmark for individual achievement in the field.

Technical Analysis Today

Today, the current technical analysis landscape is dominated primarily by automated (or systems) trading, which is an umbrella term for trading that is performed by computer systems without any continuous human input or interference. Many individual retail traders in all the major financial markets continue to trade in a manual, nonautomated fashion, but automated trading is the norm for financial institutions as well as for an ever-growing population of individual traders. These traders use a clear-cut, rules-based approach when devising trading strategies to be traded automatically by computer. Some specifics of automated trading are discussed in Chapter 14, on technical trading strategies.

From the rice markets of Osaka, Japan, in the eighteenth century to the systematic trading strategies of today, technical analysis has traveled a long path but continues to thrive as a valid, logical, and ever-growing approach to trading financial markets.

Summary

This chapter provided a quick overview of some of the most important developments within the history of technical analysis, starting from the earliest known record of the discipline appearing in the early rice markets of Osaka, Japan. This is where the precursor to Japanese candlestick charting originated and where a particularly successful rice merchant was able to profit by using pioneering financial charting techniques.

The advent of Western technical analysis can be attributed to Dow theory, a groundbreaking set of concepts originated by Charles Dow that created the framework for technical analysis as we know it today.

One of the most significant developments within the history of technical analysis has been the use of charting. Charts are the primary tool for virtually all technical analysts today. Several different types of charts developed at different times in the history of technical analysis.

These include point-and-figure charts, bar charts, and candlestick charts.

After Dow theory built the foundation, other pioneering analysts and traders emerged to augment the rapidly growing body of technical analysis knowledge. Elliott Wave theory was one of the most prominent developments, as were some of the theories put forth by W. D. Gann. Other pioneers developed and introduced indicators and oscillators that are still in heavy use today. These include RSI, stochastics, MACD, Bollinger Bands, ATR, ADX, CCI, and many more. Yet other technical analysis pioneers practiced and promoted the principles of trend following, which ultimately produced a substantial number of well-known trading successes.

The Market Technicians Association, or MTA, has been pivotal in its efforts to standardize the concepts and practices of technical analysis as well as to provide a benchmark for individual achievement in the field through its Chartered Market Technician (CMT) designation.

Today, a good portion of technical analysis and trading is performed with the use of computers. Automated and systems trading has become the norm for many institutional and individual traders. This "trend" of progressively greater trading automation promises to continue into the future.

CHAPTER 3

The Power of Technical Analysis
Principles of Price Action

After reading this chapter, you will be able to:

- Assess the sheer importance of price action and how it forms the backbone of technical analysis.

- Understand how human nature and psychology drive market price action.

- Appreciate which technical tools, methods, and concepts most effectively apply price action analysis in any given financial market.

Introduction to Price Action Concepts

Throughout the history of technical analysis, one primary unifying theme has been the foundation of this financial discipline. That theme is price action. This term may hold different meanings for different people, but many technical analysts would agree that "price action" refers to the patterned behavior of price, which can give clues to potential future direction.

As Charles Dow and his followers asserted so long ago, technical analysis purists believe that external forces, such as news events, economic conditions, and market perceptions and emotions, are all reflected in price action. Therefore, there is really no need to study all of those external forces. All market knowledge can be derived by studying price action alone.

There are countless external forces at work that can potentially affect a market's price. At any given time, deciphering exactly which combination of these forces will affect price the most, and in which direction, is extremely difficult. Therefore, technical analysts generally do not concern themselves with finding out why a market may move in a certain direction. More important than "why" is "how." Discerning the "hows" is potentially much more profitable than pondering the "whys." Through price action analysis, technical analysis gives clues as to how price may move and react in the future, based on study of price action in the past and present.

Studying price action entails studying how price in a given financial market moves according to mass human behavior. Any major financial market can generally be characterized as a mass of human beings acting out their emotions through the acts of buying and selling. Of course, this is a gross oversimplification of the financial markets, but it will suffice for the purposes of describing price action analysis.

The emotions that are acted out by these human beings while buying and selling are of many different varieties, including the primary market emotions of greed and fear. Additionally, general mass market sentiments and perceptions such as optimism and pessimism are also reflected in price action.

All of these human emotions and perceptions put together, through continuous acts of buying and selling, culminate in the price action that can be seen on any financial market chart. The ways in which this action is represented on a price chart include the primary technical analysis phenomena of trend, support and resistance, and chart patterns. All of these components of price action will be discussed in depth in later chapters.

Components of Price Action

Trend is perhaps the most salient aspect of price action. Technical analysts have always classified markets as trending up, trending down, or not trending at all. This last condition can also be regarded as trending sideways, or horizontally. Financial markets tend to trend because of the human nature inherent in the markets. Under normal circumstances, a trending market should continue to trend, until a strong enough catalyst emerges to prompt the trend to end and either begin reversing or consolidating. Higher lows and higher highs are the norm for uptrends, while downtrends are characterized by price action that makes lower highs and lower lows.

Like trend, support and resistance are also primary principles of price action. Support can be considered a floor for price action, while resistance can be considered a ceiling for price action. Of course, both a floor and a ceiling can be broken. Support and resistance, as key price action concepts, stem from the collective perceptions of market participants regarding the relative highness or lowness of certain price levels. These perceptions are manifested as price reactions to these levels, which can be used to find potential trading opportunities.

Chart patterns are simply price action formations on a chart that take on the form of certain shapes. Examples include triangles, rectangles, flags, pennants, double tops, and head and shoulders, among many others. Most chart patterns can be viewed as consolidations, where price, or the mass market, has decided to slow down and take a low-volatility breather. For most consolidations, the best potential trading opportunity exists on a strong breakout of the consolidation. For example, a common consolidative chart pattern like a triangle is really useful only after price action breaks out strongly in either direction, whether to the upside or to the downside. Before that time, not much can be done with a triangle because it is still in the process of forming.

Although many other tools are used within the field of technical analysis, such as indicators, oscillators, moving averages, and so on, these do not necessarily also belong under the umbrella of price action analysis. Most indicators and oscillators are generally just mathematically derived representations of price itself. Therefore, while they can often be pivotal in helping to formulate trading decisions, studying them is not really considered to be price action analysis. As this is the case, some traders refer to pure price action trading as "naked" trading, or trading that is devoid of mathematically derived indicators and oscillators.

The Self-Fulfilling Prophecy

The self-fulfilling prophecy plays a significant role in technical analysis. One of the key reasons that many aspects of technical analysis, especially such important concepts as support and resistance, trend lines, Fibonacci levels, and chart patterns, often seem to work remarkably well has much to do with this phenomenon. A self-fulfilling prophecy is a forecast or prediction that causes itself to become true simply because of the collective reaction to the forecast.

In the case of technical analysis, a certain support or resistance level may be validated and respected to a significant extent simply because that level is well known and is therefore watched and acted on by a critical mass of traders. So, for example, a 38.2 percent Fibonacci level, an R1 pivot point, and a key-uptrend support line do not in themselves really have magical predictive properties. It is more the fact these levels are often widely known and universally accepted, and therefore closely watched and traded by so many traders, that they often take on considerable price action significance.

Understanding the role of the self-fulfilling prophecy as a component of mass trader psychology is one of the keys to understanding the effectiveness of technical analysis in the financial markets.

Price action analysis is so powerful because it describes mass market behavior using just patterned price movements on a chart. The underlying premise of price action analysis, and of technical analysis as a whole, is that human nature and collective market behavior remain relatively consistent through time. In other words, history tends to repeat itself, at least in terms of the way people perceive, act, and react in the financial markets.

Therefore, every new trend, support/resistance level, and chart pattern tells a story that has been told time and time again. Any technical analyst or trader who has studied a major financial market for a long period of time has seen how the story tends to play out on countless occasions. Because of this fact, an experienced technical trader studying a market's price action closely can make reasonable judgments as to how price may act and react based on certain observed tendencies of mass market behavior.

As shown in the next several chapters of this book, the careful study of price action in any major financial market can make the difference between success and failure in trading.

Summary

This chapter covered the important concepts of price action. "Price action" refers to the patterned behavior of a market's price movement. The primary components of price action analysis include trend, support and resistance, and chart patterns. Other aspects of technical analysis, including chart indicators and oscillators, are not considered components of price action, as they do not represent price action itself but are instead mathematical derivatives of price.

CHAPTER 4

The Basics of Technical Analysis

Bars, Candlesticks, Lines, and Point and Figure

 After reading this chapter, you will be able to:

- Discern the differences among bar charts, candlestick charts, line charts, and point-and-figure charts.
- Recognize the basic structures and uses of all these primary charting types.
- Identify the unique structure of point-and-figure charts and how they differ fundamentally from the other charting methods.

Bars and Candlesticks

The most basic, and certainly the most important, tool of technical analysis is the price chart, which is an illuminating representation of price action for any given trading or investment instrument. The essential function of a price chart is to lay out the shape of price movement over time. This, in turn, helps technical analysts to project and/or react to likely future price behavior.

The way in which price action is structured on a chart can take several different forms. The most common methods in use today are the bar chart and the candlestick chart. Other commonly used methods include the line chart and the point-and-figure chart. Less common methods include Japanese charting methods, such as Heikin-Ashi, Renko, and three-line break.

By far, the vast majority of technical analysts and technical traders use either bars or candlesticks to depict price action on their charts. The basic structures of bars and candlesticks are very similar. They both provide the exact same information: the open price, the high price, the low price, and the close price of a given security within a given time period. This is often described as OHLC, for Open, High, Low, and Close.

As shown in Exhibit 4.1, all bar and candlestick charts have two axes—the x-axis and the y-axis. The x-axis, or the horizontal axis, represents time. It reads from left to right as time progresses. The y-axis, or the vertical axis, represents price. It is ordered from lower prices toward the bottom to higher prices toward the top.

Within this context, each bar or candlestick on a daily time frame chart, for example, will display at what price the day opened, the high

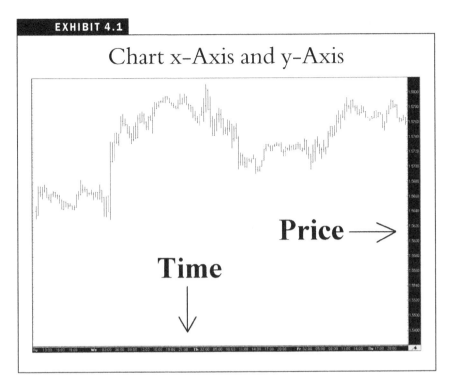

EXHIBIT 4.1

Chart x-Axis and y-Axis

Source: FX Solutions—FX AccuCharts

price of the day, the low price of the day, and at what price the day closed. When a large number of these bars or candlesticks are shown on a chart, technical traders and analysts can begin to identify patterns that may help give clues as to potential future price behavior.

While the elements of price information provided by bars and candlesticks are identical, their visual representations differ significantly. For this reason, some technical traders prefer bars, while others prefer candlesticks.

The bar chart has long been a staple of technical analysis in Western financial markets. The structure of an OHLC bar is very clear and simple, as shown in Exhibit 4.2.

EXHIBIT 4.2

Bar Structure and Candlestick Structure

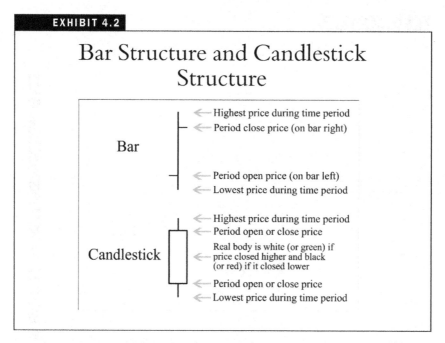

Source: FX Solutions—FX AccuCharts

Price opens the bar on the left arm and closes it on the right arm. In between, the highest price of the period is depicted by the high point of the bar, while the lowest price of the period is depicted by the low point of the bar. A bar can represent any period of time, whether it is a month, a week, a day, an hour, a minute, a series of ticks (market movements), or anything in between. Whatever time frame a bar represents, its physical appearance and structure remain constant.

The structure of candlestick charts is significantly different from bar charts. Candlesticks, as a financial analysis tool, were introduced relatively recently to the Western world from their origins in the historical rice trading markets in Japan. Steve Nison, a prominent U.S. technical analyst, was responsible for bringing this ancient yet innovative Japanese chart-reading technique to Western investors. Nison was so successful in propagating the Japanese method of candlestick charting that it arguably has superseded the popularity of bar charts in some markets.

As mentioned earlier, candlestick charts contain all of the same vital price elements contained in bar charts. The only difference lies in the visual representation of these elements. Included with the simple representation of price in candlesticks is an entire repertoire of colorfully named candlestick patterns that provide potential indications and confirmations of possible future price behavior. These patterns are covered in detail in Chapter 8, on chart patterns.

The physical structure of a candlestick appears much like a candlestick in the nonfinancial context. (See Exhibit 4.2.)

The candle body represents the prices between the candle's open and close, and the wicks (or shadows) represent the high and low extremes where price traveled during the duration of the candle.

As noted, all of the same price information contained in bars is available within the candlesticks, namely, a given period's open, high, low, and close.

While the majority of today's technical analysts and traders will turn to either bars or candlesticks to obtain vital information on the OHLC prices, some traders are interested only in closing prices. In these cases, all that is needed is a line chart.

Line Charts

Line charts appear just as their name suggests. A straight line connects each period closing price to form a connect-the-dots type of look and feel. (See Exhibit 4.3.)

EXHIBIT 4.3

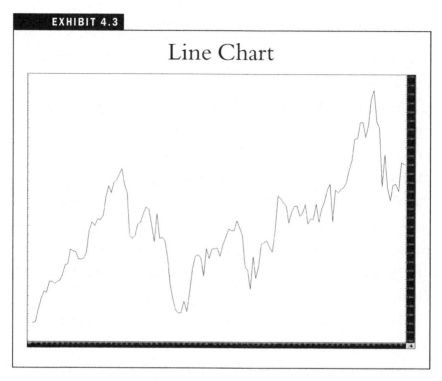

Line Chart

Like bars and candlesticks, line charts can be used with any time frame, including periods of a month, a week, a day, four hours, one hour, five minutes, one minute, and everything in between. If, for example, a five-minute chart is used, the line chart connects the closing prices of each five-minute period from left to right as time progresses. This provides a clear and simple visual depiction of price that traders who only need closing price data often prefer.

Point-and-Figure Charts

The last major chart type to be discussed here represents a marked departure from the standard bar, candlestick, and line charts. Point-

and-figure (p&f) charts differ substantially from other types of charts, and many traders who are accustomed to bars and candlesticks find it very difficult to get used to p&f charts.

The physical structure of p&f charts is characterized by alternating columns of Xs and Os, as shown in Exhibit 4.4. A column of Xs means that price went up in that particular column. Conversely, a column of Os means that price went down in that particular column.

The alternating columns of Xs and Os move from left to right as price action progresses. Unlike bars, candlesticks, and lines, however, there is a conspicuous lack of any delineated time element. In other words, time does not move the chart from left to right as in the other

EXHIBIT 4.4

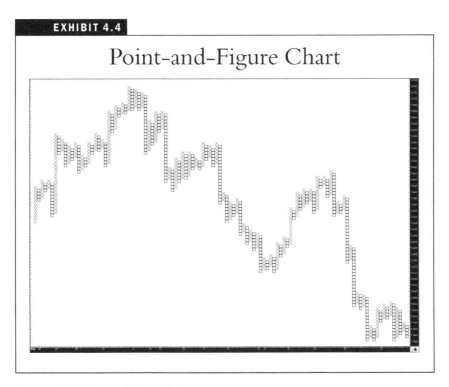

Point-and-Figure Chart

Source: FX Solutions—FX AccuCharts

chart types. The p&f chart progresses from left to right only through the movement of price. If price does not move by a minimum increment, the chart does not move. For this reason, many traders familiar with p&f charts consider them the purest form of technical analysis, as they are based exclusively on price action.

Whichever method of visually representing price action that one ultimately chooses, whether it is a bar chart, a candlestick chart, a line chart, or a point-and-figure chart, the goal is the same. All traders employing technical analysis tools in the form of charts are attempting to extrapolate potential future price behavior by graphically interpreting past and current price behavior.

The next few chapters take the technical analysis chart basics learned in this chapter and begin to apply them to real-world analysis of financial markets. The first application will be the definition and identification of trends: uptrends and downtrends.

Summary

This chapter introduced charts, which serve as the primary tool of technical analysts, as well as the major chart types. This includes bars, candlesticks, lines, and point and figure.

Bars and candlesticks are the most common chart types, by far. These types contain essentially the same information, namely O (Open), H (High), L (Low), and C (Close) prices. Line charts connect the dots of closing prices. Point-and-figure charts are a completely different method of charting prices that focuses on price action alone, to the exclusion of time. All of these charting types have their own strengths and uses, and all have their own substantial followings of technical analysts and traders.

CHAPTER 5

The Heart of Technical Analysis
Uptrends and Downtrends

After reading this chapter, you will be able to:

- Understand perhaps the most important concept within technical analysis: the concept of trend.

- Know how trends are defined and structured from a technical analysis perspective.

- Appreciate the differences between parallel trend channels and simple uptrend/downtrend lines.

- Recognize the way in which charting time frames affect how trends are assessed.

Introduction to Trend

The most essential concept in the extensive body of knowledge known as technical analysis is the idea of trend. A financial trend loosely mirrors the phenomenon in physics known as inertia, where an object in motion tends to carry the momentum to stay in motion. By the same token, if prices are going up, they tend to continue going up. And if prices are going down, they tend to continue going down.

Of course, if prices could be predicted as easily as one might predict the path of an object moving along an unobstructed, frictionless

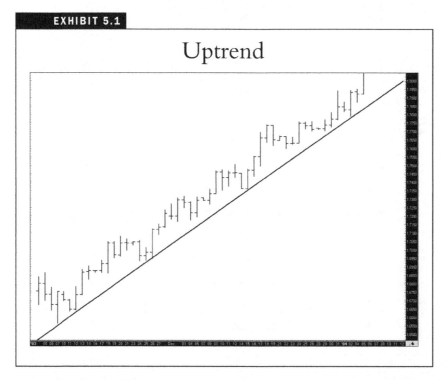

EXHIBIT 5.1

Uptrend

Source: FX Solutions—FX AccuCharts

path, there would be no need for this book. As it is, however, predicting a price path is anything but easy.

Most often, a trend will move along an irregular, jagged, zigzag path that can sometimes be difficult to discern as a trend at all. There are, however, basic guidelines as to the definition of a trend.

There are three simple variations of trend: uptrend, downtrend, and no trend. Ideally, on a bar or candlestick chart (as covered in Chapter 4), an uptrend should consist of price making higher lows and higher highs. Conversely, a downtrend should consist of price making lower highs and lower lows. (See Exhibits 5.1 and 5.2 for ideal examples.)

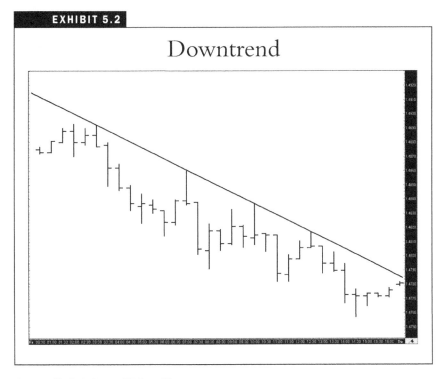

EXHIBIT 5.2

Source: FX Solutions—FX AccuCharts

EXHIBIT 5.3

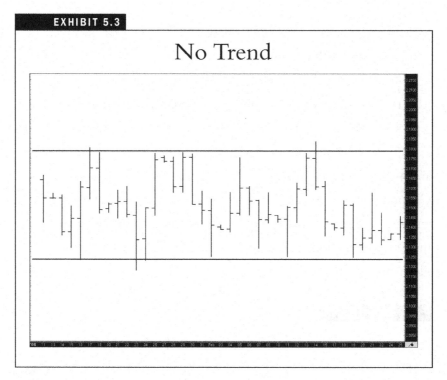

Source: FX Solutions—FX AccuCharts

Often there is no trend at all. This occurs when price moves sideways within a horizontal range, or if price action is choppy without any discernible direction. (See Exhibit 5.3 for an example.)

The basic structure of an ideal trend is perhaps best described by one of the major theories within technical analysis, Elliott Wave theory (discussed in greater detail in Chapter 11). This concept can be rather complex at its higher levels, but its basic representation of trend structure is simple and elegant.

According to Elliott Wave theory, trends are composed of two types of price movement, called waves. The first type is the motive wave, which represents the prevailing trend. The second type is the corrective wave, which moves in a countertrend fashion and retraces only a portion of the motive wave. Essentially, a trend is simply price alternating between moving in the prevailing motive direction (with the trend) and moving in the opposite corrective direction (against the trend), but with an important condition. If a trend is indeed in place, price must necessarily be making greater net progress in the prevailing direction than in the opposite direction.

This concept is akin to taking two steps forward and one step back, or, in the case of Elliott Wave, three steps forward and two steps back. The fascinating and useful concepts of Elliott Wave theory are discussed in detail in Chapter 11, which covers both Elliott Wave and Fibonacci theories.

EXECUTIVE INSIGHT

Michael Covel

In a written interview with the author, Michael Covel shares his expertise on investing versus trading and the effectiveness of nonpredictive, trend-following technical analysis. Covel is the bestselling author of *Trend Following: How Great Traders Make Millions in Up or Down Markets* (FT Press) and *The Complete Turtle Trader: The Legend, the Lessons, the Results* (HarperCollins) as well as director of the film *Broke: The New American Dream*. He is also founder of the renowned TurtleTrader.com web site and one of the most prominent authorities on trading using the trend-following approach.

Covel states:

> Do you consider yourself an investor or a trader? Most people think of themselves as investors. However, if you knew that the biggest winners in the markets call themselves traders,

wouldn't you want to know why? Simply put, they don't invest; they trade.

Investors put their money, or capital, into a market, such as stocks or real estate, under the assumption that the value will always increase over time. As the value increases, so does the person's "investment." Investors typically do not have a plan for when their investment value decreases. They usually hold on to their investment, hoping that the value will reverse itself and go back up. Investors typically succeed in bull markets and lose in bear markets.

This is because investors anticipate bear (down) markets with fear and trepidation, and, therefore, they are unable to plan how to respond when they start to lose. They choose to "hang tight," and they continue to lose. They have an idea that a different approach to their losing involves more complicated trading techniques such as "selling short," of which they know little and don't care to learn. If the mainstream press continually positions investing as "good" or "safe" and trading as "bad" or "risky," people are reluctant to align themselves with traders or even seek to understand what trading is about.

A trader has a defined plan or strategy to put capital into a market to achieve a single goal: profit. Traders don't care what they own or what they sell as long as they end up with more money than they started with. They are not investing in anything. They are trading. It is a critical distinction.

Tom Basso, a longtime trader, has said that a person is a trader whether or not he is actually trading. Some people think they must be in and out of the markets every day to call themselves traders. What makes someone a trader has more to do with his perspective on life than making a given trade. For example, a great trader's perspective includes extreme patience. Like the African lion waiting for days for the right moment to strike its unsuspecting prey, a trend follower can wait weeks or months for the right trade that puts the odds on his side.

Additionally, and ideally, traders go short as often as they go long, enabling them to make money in both up and down markets. However, a majority of traders won't or can't go short. They struggle with the concept of making money when a market declines.

There are two basic theories that are used to trade in the markets. The first theory is fundamental analysis. It is the study of external factors that affect the supply and demand of a particular market. Fundamental analysis uses factors such as weather, government policy, domestic and foreign political and economic events, price-earnings ratios, and balance sheets to make buy and sell decisions. By monitoring "fundamentals" for a particular market, one can supposedly predict a change in market direction before that change has been reflected in the price of the market with the belief that [one] can then make money from that knowledge.

The vast majority of Wall Street uses fundamental analysis alone. They are the academics, brokers, and analysts who spoke highly of the new economy during the dot-com craze. These same Wall Street players brought millions of players into the real estate and credit bubbles of 2008. Millions bought into their rosy fundamental projections and rode bubbles straight up with no clue how to exit when those bubbles finally burst.

Predictions based off of fundamental analysis don't work for the vast majority of market participants. On top of not being able to predict, fundamental analysis leaves many with trying to pick bottoms or trust that conditions will always improve. One of the great traders of the twentieth century, Ed Seykota, nailed the problem with fundamental analysis: "One evening, while having dinner with a fundamentalist, I accidentally knocked a sharp knife off the edge of the table. He watched the knife twirl through the air, as it came to rest with the pointed end sticking into his shoe. 'Why didn't you move your foot?' I exclaimed. 'I was waiting for it to come back up,' he replied." Don't we all know an investor who is waiting for 'his' market to come back?

A second market theory, technical analysis, operates in stark contrast to fundamental analysis. This approach is based on the belief that at any given point in time, market prices reflect all known factors affecting supply and demand for that particular market. Instead of evaluating fundamental factors, technical analysis looks at the market prices themselves. Technical traders believe that a careful analysis of daily price action is an effective means of trading for profit.

EXECUTIVE INSIGHT (CONTINUED)

Now, here is where an understanding of technical analysis becomes complicated. There are essentially two forms of technical analysis. One form is based on an ability to "read" charts and use "indicators" to predict market direction. This is the view of technical analysis held by most people who know of technical analysis that it is some form of mysterious chart reading technique, such as astrology.

However, there is another type of technical analysis that neither tries to predict or forecast. This type is based on reacting to price action. Trend followers are the group of technical traders who use reactive technical analysis. Instead of trying to predict a market direction, their strategy is to react to the market's movements whenever they occur. This enables them to focus on the market's actual moves and not get emotionally involved with trying to predict direction or duration.

That said, this type of price analysis never allows trend followers to enter at the exact bottom of a trend or exit at the exact top of the trend. Second, with price analysis, they don't necessarily trade every day. Instead, trend followers wait patiently for the right market conditions instead of forcing the market. Third, there should be no performance goals with price analysis. Some traders might embrace a strategy that dictates, for example, "I must make $400 dollars a day." Trend followers would counter with "Sure, but what if the markets don't move on a given day?"

One trend follower summarized the conundrum: "I could not analyze 20 markets fundamentally and make money. One of the reasons [trend following] works is because you don't try to outthink it. You are a trend follower, not a trend predictor."

A great example: The world changed in October 2008. Stock markets crashed. Millions of people lost trillions of dollars when long-held buy-and-hold strategies imploded. The Dow, Nasdaq, and S&P fell like stones, with the carnage carrying over to November 2008 and into January 2009. Most everyone has felt the ramifications: jobs lost, firms going under, and fear all around.

Clearly, no one made money during this time. Everyone lost. Hold on, is that really true? It is not. Wall Street is famous for corporate collapses or mutual fund and hedge fund blow-ups that transfer capital from winners to losers and back again. However, interestingly, the winners always seem to be missing from the after-the-fact analysis of the mainstream media. The press is fascinated with losers. Taking their lead from the press, the public also gets caught up in the drama and narrative of the losers, oblivious to the real story: Who are the winners and why? The performance histories of trend followers during the 2008 market crash, 2000–2002 stock market bubble collapse, the 1998 Long-Term Capital Management crisis, and the Barings Bank bust in 1995, answer that all important question: "Who won?"

There were winners during October 2008, and they made fortunes ranging from 5% to 40% in that single month. Many made over 100% for 2008. Who were the winners? They were trend followers.

How did they make that money? First, let me state how they did not make money:

1. They did not know stock markets would crash in October 2008.

2. They did not make all of their money from shorting stocks in 2008.

What did they do? Trend followers made money from many different markets, from oil to bonds to currencies to stocks to commodities, by following trends up and down. Trend followers always do particularly well in times of wild and extended price swings, in part because trend-following trading systems programmed into computers can make calculated, emotionless buys and sells that human traders might be slower to accept. Consider a thought about "trend" from noted trend follower Ed Seykota:

All trends are historical, none are in the present. There is no way to determine the current trend, or even define what current trend might mean; we can only determine historical trends. The only way to measure a now-trend (one entirely in the moment of now) would be to take two points, both in the now and compute their difference. Motion, velocity and trend do not exist in the now. They do not appear in snapshots. Trend does not exist

EXECUTIVE INSIGHT (CONTINUED)

in the now and the phrase "the trend" has no inherent mean-ing. . . . There is no such thing as a current trend. When we speak of trends we are necessarily projecting our own defini-tions. With that in mind, we can proceed to examine ways to define, compute and use trends.

The market crash of 2008 offered fantastic evidence to show how the trend following mind-set is so different from most of the investing world's mind-set. There are quite a few people who don't get that trend following is a trading strategy that has a track record over many traders over many different markets with thousands upon thousands of trades going back decades.

The biggest thing I have learned about the subject of trend fol-lowing over the last decade is that so many people simply either can't or won't wrap their arms around it. I can under-stand that. For 25 years Wall Street has plowed millions upon millions of investors into buy and hold and mutual funds, and when that bubble burst, fear, confusion, and debate were not surprising. Money-making literacy, or financial literacy, if you will, is clearly at a low point in the U.S.

Bottom line, even if you had never heard of trend following be-fore today, I want you to have a take away that makes sense, a take away that you can use immediately. Lesson number one for trend-following traders is: Lose the least. Trend followers won the most in 2008 by making sure they always lose the least. Think about it.

Effect of Time Frames on Trend Determination

One of the major complexities involved in determining whether there is a current trend, and if so, which direction is prevailing, has to do with time frames. Different time frames often show evidence of different trending conditions. For example, the daily chart might show a strong uptrend, while the one-hour chart shows a clear down-trend and the five-minute chart shows a consolidation that currently lacks any trend at all. In this type of situation where different time frames are giving mixed signals, which is a very frequent occurrence, how is one to label the "trend"?

The answer depends entirely on which time frame(s) a particular trader is accustomed to trading. It may well be true that the longer time frames offer more reliable trend indications, as shorter time frames tend to include a lot of market noise, or minor price fluctuations that have very little to do with the overall trend. At the same time, however, a short-term intraday trader might well be advised to ignore price action on the weekly chart entirely, as the long-term trend is virtually irrelevant to the shortest-term intraday trader. Likewise, a long-term position trader can certainly ignore the intraday price movements on the five-minute chart, as such granularity is of little use to a trader who holds positions for days, weeks, and even months.

One potential method to deal with trends as they relate to differing time frames is to concentrate on the trend indicated by a time frame four to six times longer than the one traded. For example, if a trader is accustomed to analyzing a 1-hour chart for trades, the 4-hour chart (four times the length of the 1-hour chart) could be used to indicate the prevailing trend. If a trader is accustomed to analyzing a 10-minute chart for day-to-day trading, the 1-hour chart (six times the length of the 10-minute chart) could be used to indicate the dominant trend. Finally, if a trader is accustomed to analyzing a daily chart for trades, the weekly chart (five times the length of the daily chart) could be used to indicate the trend. This four-to-six-times-higher time frame methodology should help alleviate confusion caused by conflicting trend signals on different time frames.

Parallel Trend Channels

As stated earlier, an ideal uptrend is customarily defined in the accumulated body of technical analysis knowledge as price action that makes higher highs and higher lows. Likewise, a downtrend is defined as price action that makes lower lows and lower highs. The operative term here, however, is "ideal." It is not extremely often that financial market trends act out the ideal. If they do, they often form what is referred to as a parallel trend channel.

This highly useful and revealing chart pattern is formed by two parallel lines bordering price action, one on the top and the other on the bottom. A parallel uptrend channel slopes up and borders higher lows as well as higher highs, as in Exhibit 5.4. Similarly, a parallel downtrend channel slopes down and borders lower highs as well as lower lows, as in Exhibit 5.5. These types of trend patterns therefore contain both a dynamic support element as well as a dynamic resistance element.

Within an established parallel uptrend channel, where price has touched the lower support line at least twice, subsequent bounces up off the lower support line are most often considered opportunities to buy into the uptrend. The upper resistance line of the same uptrend channel often serves as a potential profit target for those buy trades.

Similarly, in an established parallel downtrend channel, where price has touched the upper resistance line at least twice, subsequent bounces down off the upper resistance line are considered opportunities to sell (short) into the downtrend. The lower support line of the same downtrend channel often serves as a potential profit target for those short trades.

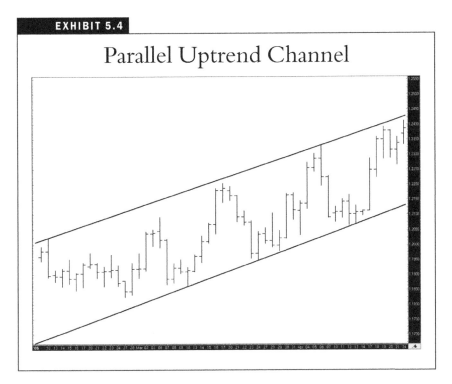

EXHIBIT 5.4

Parallel Uptrend Channel

Source: FX Solutions—FX AccuCharts

Within these parallel trend channels, the upper resistance line on an uptrend channel is sometimes considered by traders as an area to enter a sell (short) trade, and the lower support line on a downtrend channel is sometimes considered by traders as an area to enter a buy trade. The fact that these types of entries represent clear countertrend trades, however, make them less appealing to those traders looking to stay consistently with the trend.

As mentioned earlier, financial markets do not always manifest the ideal pattern when it comes to trend activity. Finding parallel trend channels with regular higher highs and higher lows for

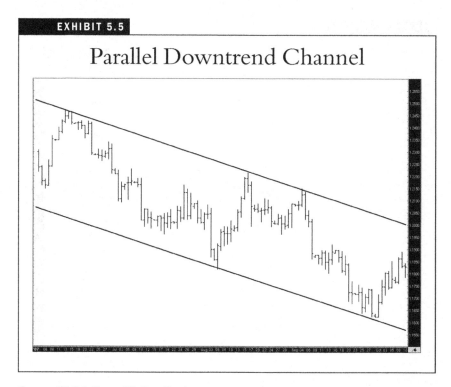

EXHIBIT 5.5

Parallel Downtrend Channel

uptrends, and regular lower lows and lower highs for downtrends, is often difficult.

Trend Lines

Much easier to find in any financial market is price action that depicts just higher lows in an uptrend or just lower highs in a downtrend. The trend patterns for these are called uptrend support lines and downtrend resistance lines, respectively. These trend lines are the primary drawing tool for technical analysts and traders in any financial market to depict and measure trends. They are one of the key work-horses in the technical trader's arsenal that often describe trending price action in a remarkably accurate manner.

Specific methods for drawing trend lines and trend channels accurately are discussed in Chapter 7. For now, it should be kept in mind that trends are a very real phenomenon in all financial markets, whether it is stocks, bonds, futures, or foreign exchange. This is due primarily to the fact that mass human psychology drives all of these markets. This human factor sustains trends long after they should have reasonably ended, and it is also the driving force behind the critically important concepts of support and resistance, which together form the soul of technical analysis. This is the topic for Chapter 6.

Summary

This chapter introduced the heart of technical analysis: trends. A trend can be considered directional price action, whether up or down. Trends are perhaps best described by a major theory within technical analysis called Elliott Wave theory.

The time frame that a technical analyst views will have a bearing on how that analyst assesses the prevailing trend. Looking on a longer-term time frame than that which one is trading can be helpful in determining the larger trend.

Trends that are bounded by parallel trend channels can be considered ideal trends. This is due to the fact that in a parallel uptrend channel, there are higher lows as well as higher highs. Similarly, in a parallel downtrend channel, there are lower highs as well as lower lows.

Trend lines, since they are found very often in all financial markets, are the primary workhorses for describing trends. Uptrend lines connect higher lows without connecting higher highs, while downtrend lines connect lower highs without connecting lower lows.

CHAPTER 6

The Soul of Technical Analysis

Support and Resistance

After reading this chapter, you will be able to:

- Understand the core importance of support and resistance in price action analysis.
- Define the roles of support and resistance and how they drive price pressures.
- Appreciate one of the primary tenets of technical analysis: Support tends to become resistance, and resistance tends to become support.

Introduction to Support and Resistance

Along with the concept of trend, support and resistance are at the very core of technical analysis. These twin elements of market psychology are intertwined and inseparable, and they form the essential structure of price action in all financial markets. While the basis of support and resistance is rather easy to grasp, their significance is far-reaching.

Support and resistance are two parts of one whole. They can also be considered polar opposites. Where support can be compared to a price floor, resistance can be considered a price ceiling. Support can simply be defined as the recurring upward price "pressure" exerted by expected net market buying at relatively lower prices. By the same token, resistance can be defined as the recurring downward price "pressure" exerted by expected net market selling at relatively higher prices.

These upward and downward pressures have a number of hypothetical causes, many of which can be traced back to mass trader psychology. More specifically, the existence of support and resistance levels and their often remarkable ability to describe price action stems primarily from market participants' price memory and human emotions.

From a price memory perspective, sustainable support and resistance levels will occur because traders large and small remember specific price levels and will base their trading decisions on whether they consider these levels high or low on a relative basis. The most basic tendency is for traders to buy at price levels they consider relatively low (support) and to sell at price levels they consider relatively high (resistance).

When a majority of traders, or, more accurately, a majority of trading dollars, collectively believe that a certain price level or price region is relatively low, buying pressure often results and the price should generally go up, thereby creating a bounce up off support. Conversely, when a majority of traders believe that a certain price level or region is relatively high, selling pressure often results and the price should generally go down, thereby creating a bounce down off resistance.

The general expectation at a price level that is considered collectively by traders to be relatively low (or a "floor") is that when price reaches down to that support level, it should turn and go back up. This is due to new buying around that level both by traders wishing to get into the market at a low price and traders with existing short positions who may wish to buy back (or cover) their short positions to book their profits.

Similarly, the general expectation at a price level that is considered collectively by traders to be relatively high (or a "ceiling") is that when price reaches up to that resistance level, it should turn and go back down. This is due to new selling around that level both by traders wishing to short the market at a high price and traders with existing long positions who may wish to sell their positions to book their profits.

While the expectations of price turning up at support and turning down at resistance are strong, equally significant events, from a technical analysis basis, occur when price breaks through, or violates, these levels. The theoretical logic behind breakouts is that valid support and resistance levels should normally be respected by the market. If price is able to muster the momentum to break cleanly through a significant level, it indicates that the catalyst behind such a forceful price move is potentially strong enough to drive price even further in the same direction after the breakout. This expectation fuels traders to watch for and participate in strong breakouts of established support and resistance levels. Therefore, both bounces and breakouts of support and resistance are highly anticipated events by traders in all financial markets.

The simple fact that support and resistance levels are often respected by price numerous times before ultimately being broken is, in itself, a remarkable phenomenon that can contribute a great deal to any technical trader's trading strategy. Whenever price nears historically significant support or resistance levels, traders invariably begin paying a great deal of attention to the price action, waiting for the level in question to be either respected or violated. These traders will then act accordingly by buying or selling the market, depending entirely on how price reacted to the particular support or resistance level.

Sideways price action between both a support floor and a resistance ceiling is called a trading range, as displayed in Exhibit 6.1. Trading ranges occur quite often in all financial markets. Many traders exploit such horizontal consolidation zones as range-trading opportunities where they buy near support and sell near resistance. Other traders prefer to treat these ranges as breakout trading opportunities, waiting for a breakout above the resistance ceiling or a breakdown below the support floor before getting into any trade.

Support Becomes Resistance Becomes Support

An extremely important and useful aspect of traders' collective price memory as it relates to the concept of support and resistance lies in

EXHIBIT 6.1

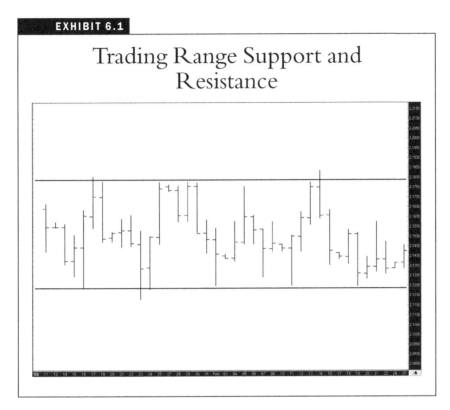

Trading Range Support and Resistance

Source: FX Solutions—FX AccuCharts

the extraordinary tendency for a support/resistance level to transform into the opposite once broken (as displayed in Exhibit 6.2). For example, when price breaks out above a resistance level, technical analysts would then consider that broken resistance level as a new support level. Similarly, when price breaks down below a support level, technical analysts would then consider that broken support level as a new resistance level. Among all other tenets of technical analysis, this is arguably one that holds exceptional weight with analysts and traders alike. This is due to the fact that the phenomenon of

EXHIBIT 6.2

Resistance Becomes Support

Source: FX Solutions—FX AccuCharts

support becoming resistance, and vice versa, manifests itself frequently on all types of financial price charts.

The most plausible reasoning behind this phenomenon, from a trader psychology perspective, is that once a currency pair breaks a support/resistance level in a convincing manner, traders begin to believe that price has reached a whole new plateau of activity.

If, for example, a key resistance level is broken out to the upside, traders who were short at the breakout, and did not close their positions, begin to panic. If price descends to the point where it broke that resistance, these traders are all too happy to get out of their trades at breakeven, or at least at a smaller loss. When these traders cover their short positions by buying back, it places significant upward price pressure right at the previous resistance level, contributing to this level's new role as support. Additionally, traders who missed getting into the breakout trade when price first broke resistance are looking to get in on the new bullishness. If price descends to the point where it broke the previous resistance, many of these traders will want to get in at this dip with long trades so that they can partake in the potential continuation of the uptrend break. This places more upward price pressure right at the previous resistance level, further contributing to this level's new role as support.

On the opposite end of the spectrum, if a key support level is broken to the downside, traders who were long at the breakdown, and did not close their positions, begin to panic. If price ascends to the point where it broke that support, these traders are all too happy to get out of their trades at breakeven, or at least at a smaller loss. When these traders sell their long positions, it places significant downward price pressure right at the previous support level, contributing to this level's new role as resistance. Additionally, traders who missed getting into the breakout trade when price first broke support are looking to get in on the new bearishness. If price ascends to the point where it broke the previous support, many of these traders will want to get in at this rally with short trades so that they can partake in the potential continuation of the downtrend break. This places more downward price pressure right at the previous support level, further contributing to this level's new role as resistance.

After a key support or resistance level is broken with strong momentum, the mass trader momentum moves away from the previous price zone and toward equilibrium at a new zone. The border between the old zone and the new zone is the broken support/resistance level, which thenceforth is expected to serve the role of a future price barrier—as support where it was previously resistance, and as resistance where it was previously support.

This principle is a central theme of support/resistance theory, which, in turn, is a central theme of technical analysis as a whole. Methods of measuring and drawing horizontal support and resistance lines are introduced in Chapter 7, which also covers the drawing of trend lines and trend channels.

Summary

This chapter introduced the soul of technical analysis: support and resistance. These twin concepts form the backbone of technical analysis in the media as well as in practical technical trading by many traders and investors. Support acts as a price "floor" providing upward pressure, while resistance acts as a price "ceiling" providing downward pressure. These concepts work because of mass trader psychology.

Traders will often either trade bounces off these levels or breakouts of these levels. Sideways price action between support and resistance is called a trading range.

An important principle of technical analysis is that support, after being broken, tends to become resistance. In the same way, resistance, after being broken, tends to become support. This phenomenon, like that of support/resistance as a whole, is based on mass trader psychology.

CHAPTER 7

Primary Drawing Tools
Trend Lines, Trend Channels, and Horizontal Support and Resistance

After reading this chapter, you will be able to:

- Understand how the primary chart drawing tools, including trend lines, trend channels, and horizontal support/resistance lines, are used effectively.

- Know how these lines are structured and drawn by technical analysts.

- Identify exactly how technical traders use these drawn lines to trade their chosen financial markets.

Introduction to Drawing Tools

Trend lines, trend channels, and horizontal support and resistance lines are among the most basic, but also among the most powerful, tools in the technical analyst's toolbox. Over decades of new techniques and developments in technical analysis, the simplest line drawings have remained one of the primary cornerstones of the craft.

Trend lines, trend channels, and horizontal lines are the primary tools for representing the two general forms of support and resistance: static and dynamic.

Before going into a detailed description of methods for drawing static and dynamic support/resistance levels on charts, it should be noted from the outset that support and resistance lines and levels rarely exhibit the precision that many people may expect or wish for. Because support and resistance are represented on charts by rather clear-cut straight lines, many traders who are new to technical analysis mistakenly have the impression that price should turn precisely at a specific price level. Or they believe that if price breaks a certain established support or resistance level by only a minimum price increment, a bona fide breakout has occurred. This could not be further from the truth.

Support and resistance should more accurately be described as regions or zones around which market activity reacts. Rarely does price action obey established support/resistance levels as precisely as one would hope. At the same time, though, this fact does not in any way make support and resistance devoid of usefulness for the experienced technical trader. On the contrary, awareness of a price region where there is a high probability of a market reaction is powerful knowledge that can be used to a trader's substantial benefit. Although usually far from precise, this type of market insight can and does produce consistent trading profits for many traders in all of the various financial markets.

Static Support and Resistance

To return to the delineation between static and dynamic support/resistance, static levels are price levels that do not change. This is not to say that a static level never loses its relevance or validity. On the contrary, many historical support and resistance levels lose their usefulness over time as price action develops, and these levels often become forgotten. But during the time that a static level is valid, its price does not change. The most prominent example of a static level is a price level where price turned, or reversed, at least once in the past, but preferably more frequently. One key tenet of technical analysis, as it relates to support and resistance, is that the more times price reverses at or around a given price level, the stronger that price becomes as static support or resistance. See Exhibits 7.1 and 7.2 for static support and resistance examples.

Among the strongest levels to establish major support or resistance are long-term historical highs or lows, including all-time price highs or lows. From a price memory perspective, traders collectively remember extreme levels like these better than they do other, less prominent price levels. As a result, when current price action returns to these levels, market reactions tend to be clearer and more pronounced, and therefore even more useful to the technical trader.

EXHIBIT 7.1

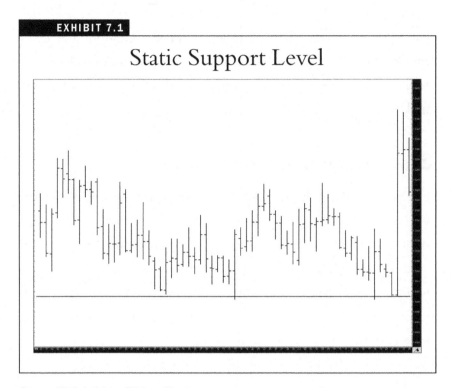

Static Support Level

Source: FX Solutions—FX AccuCharts

Besides levels where price reversed in the past, other manifestations of static support and resistance can be found in such technical forecasting tools as Fibonacci retracements and pivot points. Fibonacci theory is a complex subject that is dealt with in greater detail, along with Elliott Wave theory, in Chapter 11. For now, though, the important Fibonacci retracement tool (as shown in Exhibit 7.3) serves as a model example of static, or horizontal, support and resistance levels.

In a similar fashion, pivot points are mathematically derived static support and resistance levels used for any given trading day that are

EXHIBIT 7.2

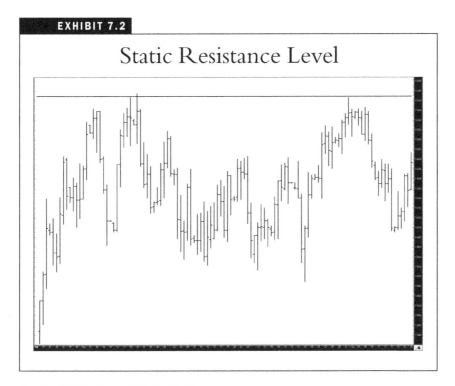

Static Resistance Level

Source: FX Solutions—FX AccuCharts

based on the prior day's high, low, and close prices. Pivot point trading has been used extensively by floor traders, and continues to be used by traders in many financial markets as a source of support/resistance reference levels. See Exhibit 7.4 for an example of pivot points plotted on a chart.

To calculate the main, central pivot point (labeled PP), for example, a trader would take the mean (average) of the previous day's high, low, and close prices. Then the trader would calculate four additional pivot points (named S1, S2, R1, and R2, where S = Support and R = Resistance) based on the central pivot point. Some traders add even

EXHIBIT 7.3

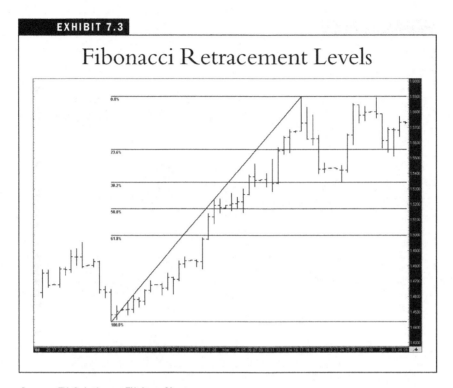

Fibonacci Retracement Levels

Source: FX Solutions—FX AccuCharts

more pivot points beyond the basic four plus the central pivot point, including S3 and R3. For the actual calculations, see the Tips and Techniques section on pivot point calculations. Some charting software packages automatically calculate pivot points and plot them on the chart so that the trader does not need to calculate them manually.

The primary concept behind pivot points is that they can act as key support and resistance levels where price may potentially turn within the course of a trading day. Traders can calculate the current day's relevant pivot points based on the previous day's price data and

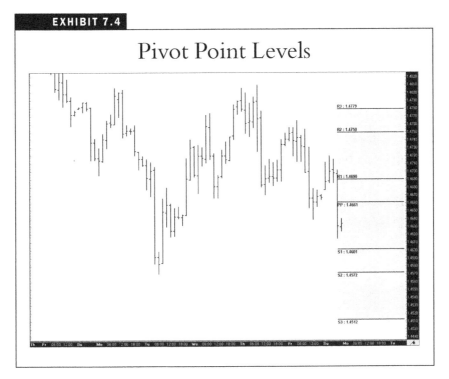

EXHIBIT 7.4

Pivot Point Levels

R3 : 1.4779

R2 : 1.4750

R1 : 1.4690

PP : 1.4661

S1 : 1.4601

S2 : 1.4572

S3 : 1.4512

Source: FX Solutions—FX AccuCharts

then plot the levels using horizontal lines on a price chart. Once these levels are calculated and plotted, breakouts and bounces can be traded, and they can also be used as profit targets for existing trades. Traders often use pivot points as reference levels to provide guidance as to whether the current price is relatively high or relatively low within its expected range for the day. If price is near the current day's S2 level, for example, traders may look for opportunities to trade long with the view that price could reasonably move toward equilibrium around the central PP level.

Daily Pivot Point Calculations

R3 (Resistance 3) = Yesterday's High + 2(PP − Yesterday's Low)

R2 (Resistance 2) = PP + (R1 − S1)

R1 (Resistance 1) = 2 × PP − Yesterday's Low

PP (Pivot Point) = (Yesterday's High + Yesterday's Low
    + Yesterday's Close) ÷ 3

S1 (Support 1) = 2 × PP − Yesterday's High

S2 (Support 2) = PP − (R1 − S1)

S3 (Support 3) = Yesterday's Low − 2(Yesterday's High − PP)

Dynamic Support and Resistance

In contrast to static price levels, dynamic support and resistance represent price levels that change over time. The best single example of dynamic levels can be found in the simple trend line.

Customarily, trend lines that go up, called uptrend lines, are measured by connecting successively higher price lows. Therefore, as shown in Exhibit 7.5, uptrend lines are often referred to as uptrend support lines, as these lines provide a dynamic, or changing, floor for price action. In an uptrend, the floor rises based on the slope of the line. An uptrend support line with a steeper slope means that price is rising at a faster rate, whereas a flatter slope means that price is rising at a slower rate.

In contrast, trend lines that go down, called downtrend lines, are measured by connecting successively lower price highs. Therefore, as shown in Exhibit 7.6, downtrend lines are often referred to as

EXHIBIT 7.5

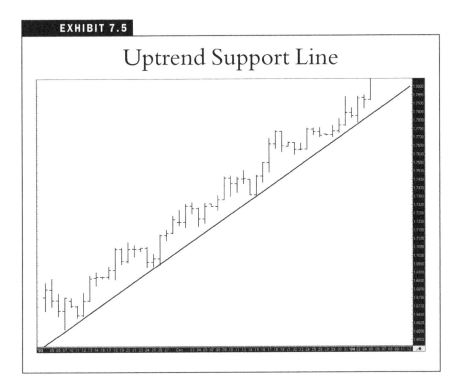

Uptrend Support Line

Source: FX Solutions—FX AccuCharts

downtrend resistance lines, as these lines provide a dynamic, or changing, ceiling for price action. In a downtrend, the ceiling falls based on the slope of the line. A downtrend resistance line with a steeper slope means that price is falling at a faster rate, whereas a flatter slope means that price is falling at a slower rate.

When connecting higher lows for a new uptrend or lower highs for a new downtrend, at least two lows or highs must exist in order to create the line, but preferably three or more. Similar to the horizontal support and resistance lines, the more price respects any given trend line, as with three or more touches, the stronger and more valid the trend line.

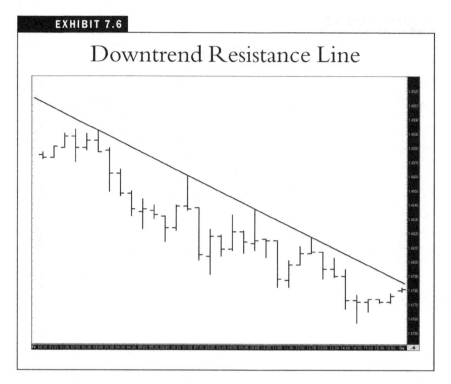

EXHIBIT 7.6

Downtrend Resistance Line

Source: FX Solutions—FX AccuCharts

The practical applications of trend lines are wide and varied. In fact, many traders prefer to use trend line analysis almost exclusively in dictating their trading decisions. Trend lines can be used to pinpoint pullback (or dip) trade entries, breakout reversal entries, and prudent stop-losses. Although there may be some subjectivity in their construction and interpretation, trend lines have withstood the test of time as an integral component of many of the most profitable, and often simplest, trading strategies.

Besides the trend line, another major form of dynamic support and resistance can be found in the parallel trend channel. If a trend line supplies just the floor for an uptrend, the parallel uptrend channel provides the ceiling as well. By the same token, if a trend line supplies just the ceiling for a downtrend, the parallel downtrend channel provides the floor as well. As mentioned in Chapter 5 on trend theory, price action that truly fits comfortably into the borders of a parallel trend channel upholds the highest ideals of a true trend. This is because, for example, an uptrend that fits well into a parallel uptrend channel will contain both higher lows and higher highs, as shown in Exhibit 7.7. Likewise, a downtrend that fits well into a parallel downtrend channel will contain both lower highs and lower lows, as shown

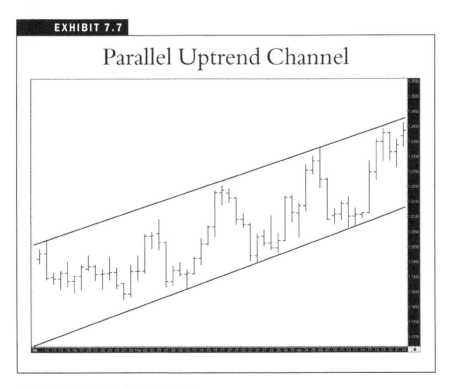

EXHIBIT 7.7

Parallel Uptrend Channel

Source: FX Solutions—FX AccuCharts

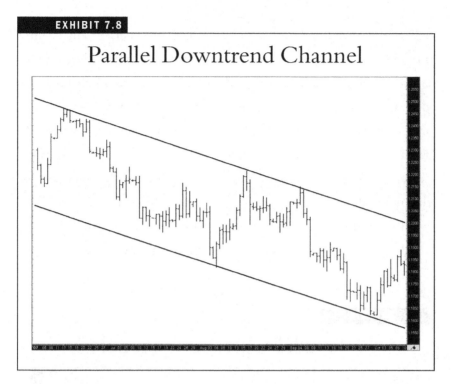

EXHIBIT 7.8

Parallel Downtrend Channel

Source: FX Solutions—FX AccuCharts

in Exhibit 7.8. This is in contrast to the single trend line, which requires price to fulfill only half the ideal.

Like its little cousin, the trend line, the parallel trend channel can be used to pinpoint pullback trade entries, breakout reversal entries, and prudent stop-losses. Additionally, the line within the trend channel that the single trend line lacks, often called the "return line," can be used as a profit target for trades initiated at the original trend line. For example, in a parallel uptrend channel, trades in the direction of the trend should be initiated around the original uptrend support line, the bottom border of the parallel channel. A convenient profit target for such trades would be the return line, or the top border of the parallel channel.

Before moving on to the methods for drawing the different static and dynamic lines on a chart, as well as their specific trading uses, two caveats with regard to trading parallel trend channels should be noted.

For one, these channels often encourage traders to trade against the trend. In an uptrend, for example, with support on the bottom and resistance on the top, many traders are tempted not only to enter long trades at the bottom of the channel but also to enter short trades at the top of the channel. While a long entry on the bottom of an uptrend channel is certainly a trade in the direction of the trend, a short entry at the top of that same uptrend channel constitutes a countertrend trade. Though countertrend trading is by no means a taboo practice, and it can often prove to be a profitable trading style for experienced traders, it is probably best for newer technical traders to stick to trading in a higher-probability direction—with the trend. According to strict trend traders, the top of an uptrend channel should be used exclusively for profit taking on long trades rather than entering short trades against the direction of the trend. The same holds true, but in an opposite fashion, for downtrends.

The second caveat regarding channels relates to breakouts. Many novice traders will treat breakouts on both sides of a trend channel as similar events. This is an erroneous assumption. In a parallel uptrend channel, for example, a breakdown below the uptrend support line of the channel represents a potential trend reversal that is generally considered a highly significant and potentially actionable event. A breakout above the top line of the uptrend channel, however, is much less of an important or actionable event from a trading perspective. This type of breakout merely represents an acceleration of the existing uptrend, which is important information in itself but is not the groundbreaking news that a true breakdown reversal would represent. Again, this caveat holds equally true, but in an opposite fashion, for downtrend channels.

Now that the tools and definitions for both static and dynamic support/resistance have been established, the methods for drawing these lines, and their specific uses, can be discussed.

Horizontal Support and Resistance Lines

To begin with, horizontal support and resistance lines are customarily drawn connecting the approximate highs or lows of price bars on a chart. The analyst or trader drawing these lines need not be overly concerned about being absolutely precise in plotting these lines. As mentioned earlier, price action rarely adheres to established support and resistance levels in a precise manner. As long as the lines are drawn as close to the majority of highs/lows as possible, these lines should serve as strong indicators of valid support or resistance.

Generally, a support/resistance trader will approach a blank price chart with the intention of plotting the price levels at which price seems to turn at multiple points. These multiple points could all be turns up from support, they could all be turns down from resistance, or they could be a combination of both. This combination of both types of turns is a relatively frequent occurrence since, as mentioned in Chapter 6, support often becomes resistance and resistance often becomes support.

Many technical traders approach a blank price chart beginning on the longer-term time frames, so that the major long-term support and resistance turns, or pivots, can be plotted first. Then these traders progressively drill down to shorter time frames so that more recent support and resistance pivots can then be plotted. The most recent levels would then be plotted on the shortest time frame.

All of these levels will have some significance for technical analysts. Generally speaking, however, as mentioned earlier in this chapter, long-term historical highs and lows carry substantially stronger significance. All-time highs and lows, especially, are among the most important support or resistance levels that can be plotted.

In addition, all other characteristics being equal, more recent high and low pivots tend to carry greater weight as support/resistance than those that occurred farther back in time. This stems, once again, from the price memory phenomenon. Traders naturally remember significant recent price levels much better than they do equally significant distant price levels.

Once all of these horizontal lines are plotted on a price chart, the support/resistance trader watches for price reactions at each of these levels, whether each one is respected with a bounce or violated with a break. If the trader is trading strictly with the trend, only those bounces or breaks in the direction of the prevailing trend would actually be traded. If the trader is range trading, bounces between support and resistance levels would offer trade entry opportunities. There are a multitude of ways in which technical traders approach price reactions to support and resistance, some of which are discussed in Chapter 14, on technical trading strategies.

The general concept, though, is simply to trade bounces or breaks of support or resistance levels, often using trade entry filters in an effort to avoid false bounces or breaks. An entry filter is a method for lending some confirmation that a support/resistance bounce or break is, in fact, real. For example, a trader might not trade a resistance breakout unless price action exceeds the point of break by a predetermined price increment. The same type of filter might also be used, for example, to confirm a bounce off support. Another example of an entry filter is a pullback to the point of breakout, after the breakout. Many traders will wait after a support/resistance breakout until price pulls back to the point of breakout and then resumes in the direction of the original breakout, before getting into the trade. Yet another entry filter is to wait for the breakout bar/candle to close and then for the next bar/candle to surpass the extremity of the breakout bar/candle. This provides at least some indication that momentum may be continuing in the direction of the break. Entry filters can be used with horizontal support/resistance lines as well as with dynamic levels like trend lines and trend channels.

Besides their effective use for trade entries, horizontal support/resistance levels are also one of the best references for determining optimal stop-loss exits. Whether a given support/resistance level is violated or respected, there is always a built-in, straightforward location for placing an initial stop-loss. For example, on a trade entry triggered by a breakout of resistance, the initial stop-loss would logically be placed a certain predetermined distance below the point of breakout, where the original reason for getting into the trade (a bullish breakout) would no longer be valid. Similarly, on a trade entry triggered by a bounce up off of a support line, the initial stop-loss would logically be placed a certain predetermined distance below the support line, where the original reason for getting into the trade (a bullish support bounce) would no longer be valid.

Trend Lines

Much like horizontal support and resistance lines, trend lines are also drawn to connect highs and lows. The difference, as mentioned earlier in this chapter, is that trend lines connect dynamically changing highs and lows rather than static ones.

There has been much debate over many years among technical analysts and traders as to the correct method for drawing a trend line. As a result, there are almost as many ways to draw a trend line as there are traders making trading decisions based on them.

In a clear uptrend situation, for example, some technicians connect lows from the left-hand side of the chart to the right-hand side of the chart. Others connect from right to left. In a separate disagreement, some technicians are sticklers about connecting the very low point of each pivoting bar to form the perfect uptrend line. Others connect only the "best," or most significant, lows while having their trend lines cross through intermediate bars. Their rationale is that some price bars represent anomalous spikes in price action that can essentially be considered statistical outliers, and therefore should not be included when drawing a trend line. Still other technicians prefer to concentrate on bar closing prices only, as opposed to highs or lows, when drawing trend lines. These and other debates will likely continue as long as there are markets to trade and traders to trade them. This fact accounts in part for the subjectivity involved with drawing trend lines and trend channels. Traders are simply drawing them differently.

Another issue with the drawing of trend lines is that they often have to be erased and redrawn if price action happens to invalidate them. For example, suppose that in a situation where a fresh uptrend line connects two low points, price breaks below the uptrend line, invalidating it. If price then goes on to make a new low point and then continues on up to form an uptrend, the uptrend line has to be redrawn to incorporate the new low point after the breakdown, as shown in Exhibit 7.9.

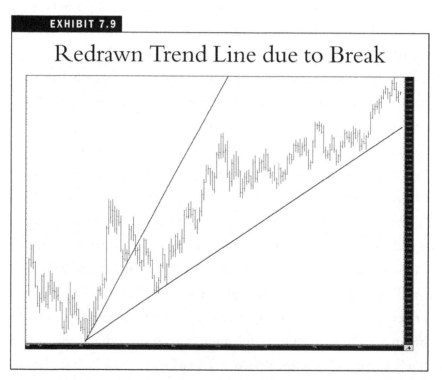

EXHIBIT 7.9

Redrawn Trend Line due to Break

Source: FX Solutions—FX AccuCharts

EXHIBIT 7.10

Redrawn Trend Line due to Trend Acceleration

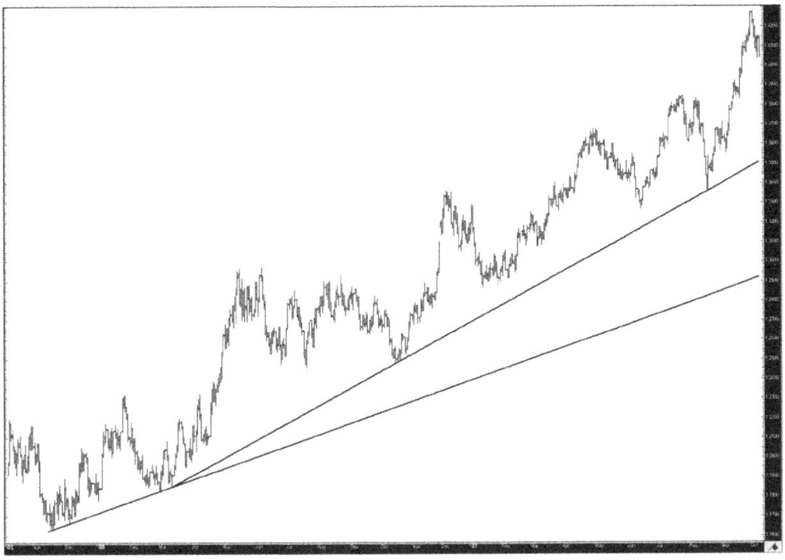

Source: FX Solutions—FX AccuCharts

Trend lines also potentially need to be redrawn if price accelerates in the direction of the prevailing trend, forming a steeper trend line (as in Exhibit 7.10).

These issues notwithstanding, trend lines still remain the best manual method for representing trends. Potential problems with subjectivity and with having to redraw lines do not take away from the fact that trend lines frequently prove to be remarkable financial forecasting tools; they have proven over the course of time to be one of the primary technical workhorses for legions of technical traders in every financial market.

Once a trend line is drawn to satisfaction, traders use it to interpret and react to price action, much as they would with horizontal support and resistance levels. Trend lines can be used for trade entries on bounces, trade entries on breaks, and logical stop-loss placement.

Bounces off trend lines are the equivalent of dips or pullbacks within the trend, excellent entry points into an established trend. These trend line bounces represent countertrend retracements within the context of the prevailing trend, which makes them high-probability areas for jumping onto a trend at attractive prices. For example, in the case of an existing uptrend, as shown in Exhibit 7.11, any touch and bounce up off the uptrend support line occurs after price has made a minor countertrend retracement. The price at, or shortly after, each dip is an optimal price for an entry, as it is a less expensive location to buy into the existing uptrend. Similarly, during a downtrend when price ascends to and then bounces lower off a downtrend resistance line, short-selling on these rallies, which are simply minor upward retracements within the overall downtrend, is a frequently used strategy for getting into an established downtrend at optimal prices.

One high-probability method of trading these bounces involves entering on breaks of countertrend trend lines, as shown in Exhibit 7.12. For example, in an uptrend situation where price has made at least two or three lows that can be connected by an uptrend support line, each subsequent low that bounces off the uptrend line presents an opportunity to buy into the uptrend at an optimal price. But where exactly should a trader enter into that trend after the bounce to have greater confidence that a continuing uptrend is

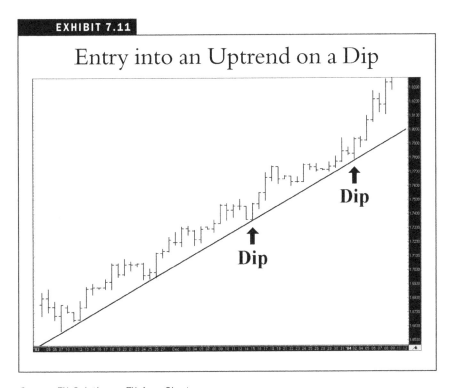

EXHIBIT 7.11

Entry into an Uptrend on a Dip

Source: FX Solutions—FX AccuCharts

indeed in place? One good way is to trade breaks of the countertrend retracements. Within the main uptrend, every time price retraces back down to the uptrend support line, a minor downtrend resistance line should be created, connecting two or more highs within the bearish retracement. After the bounce up off the main trend line occurs, any breakout above the minor downtrend resistance line can be considered a high-probability entry point into the trend. Although it may produce a later trade entry than other methods, it is a stronger confirmation that any bounce off the main trend line could potentially have continued follow-through.

EXHIBIT 7.12

Trend Line Trading on Breaks of Countertrend Lines

Source: FX Solutions—FX AccuCharts

Other than the trend line bounce, another primary trade entry event is the trend line break. Trend line breaks represent potential trend reversals and are watched very closely by technical traders. For example, in an uptrend situation where an uptrend support line connects two or more lows, a breakdown below the trend line represents an interruption in the uptrend and a possible reversal to begin a new downtrend. Of course, price could very well just consolidate or even break above the trend line again, but the anticipated outcome of a bona fide trend line break is a trend reversal. Much like when a break of horizontal support or resistance occurs, trend line breaks are often traded with an entry filter. Whether the filter used is a certain price increment beyond the point of break, or a pullback move after the break, or a new bar/candle surpassing the breakout bar/candle, many traders will want to have some additional confirmation of the trend line breakout before committing to the trade.

Also much like horizontal support and resistance levels, trend line trades always have built-in, straightforward locations for placing optimal stop-losses. For example, on a trade entry triggered by a breakdown of an uptrend support line, the initial stop-loss would logically be placed a certain predetermined distance above the trend line point of breakdown, where the original reason for getting into the trade (a bearish trend line break) would no longer be valid. Similarly, on a trade entry triggered by a bounce up off an uptrend support line, the initial stop-loss would logically be placed a certain predetermined distance below the uptrend line, where the original reason for getting into the trade (a bullish trend line bounce) would no longer be valid.

Parallel Trend Channels

Finally, we come back to the parallel trend channel, that bastion of ideal trendiness. Parallel trend channels are customarily traded in the same fashion as trend lines, with one important distinction. Channels possess built-in profit targets. For example, in a parallel uptrend channel, where price has touched the bottom support trend line and the top return line at least two times each, any subsequent long trade triggered by a bounce off the bottom support trend line should shoot for a profit target around the resistance imposed by the top return line. Many traders will actually set the profit target just short of the return line in a bid to increase the chances that the profit target is reached.

When price fails to reach the top return line in a parallel uptrend channel before turning down and heading south for the bottom support trend line, this is considered a substantially bearish indication that could presage an eventual breakdown below the uptrend channel and a potential trend reversal. Conversely, when price breaks out above the top return line in a parallel uptrend channel, it is considered a bullish acceleration of the existing uptrend that could presage a steeper uptrend, requiring a redrawing of the trend line. All of this holds true, but in the opposite fashion, for parallel downtrend channels.

As mentioned earlier in this chapter, the two caveats regarding parallel trend channel trading are worth reiterating here. First, breakouts of channels are not all created equal. On a parallel uptrend channel, a breakdown below the bottom support line is a significant event, indicating a potential trend reversal that should trigger substantial interest in short-trading the breakdown. In contrast, a breakout above the top return line simply represents a trend acceleration, which does not carry nearly as much technical significance as the main trend line break. Similarly, on a parallel downtrend channel, a breakout above the top resistance line is a significant event, indicating a potential trend reversal that should trigger substantial interest in buying the breakout. In contrast, a breakdown below the bottom return line simply represents a trend acceleration, which does not carry nearly as much technical significance as the main trend line break.

The second caveat has to do with trading on signals from the return line, which are considered countertrend trades. In a parallel uptrend channel, for example, long trades triggered by bounces up off the bottom uptrend support line are considered trades with the trend. In contrast, short trades triggered by bounces down off the top return line, which many traders may be tempted to make, are countertrend trades that carry the risks and probabilities of countertrend trading. Similarly, in a parallel downtrend channel, short trades triggered by bounces down off the top downtrend resistance line are considered trades with the trend. In contrast, long trades triggered by bounces up off the bottom return line, which many traders may be tempted to make, are countertrend trades that carry the risks and probabilities of countertrend trading.

Now that the primary drawing tools of trend lines, trend channels, and horizontal support and resistance lines have been covered, the next step is to introduce and describe the many bar and candlestick patterns available to the technical trader. This is the subject of Chapter 8.

Summary

This chapter introduced the primary drawing tools that technical analysts use on financial price charts. These tools include trend lines, trend channels, and horizontal support and resistance lines.

Static support and resistance levels are ones that do not change in price. They include simple horizontal lines where price turned or reversed in the past as well as Fibonacci levels and pivot points.

Dynamic support and resistance represent price levels that change over time. Trend lines are the best example of dynamic support and resistance, along with parallel trend channels, which are essentially dual trend lines.

In both static and dynamic support/resistance, traders generally watch for price reactions at or around these levels to see if they are respected with a bounce or violated with a break. Then trade entries can be planned and executed. Stop-losses may also be planned and executed based on the location of price in relation to the static (horizontal line) or dynamic (trend line) support/resistance level.

CHAPTER 8

Chart Patterns
Bar Shapes and Candlestick Formations

After reading this chapter, you will be able to:

- Identify the structures and characteristics of the most important bar and candlestick chart patterns.
- Understand how technical traders use these patterns to provide clues about future potential price action.
- Assess all of the practical trading aspects of these chart patterns.

Introduction to Chart Patterns

For many of those who are unfamiliar with technical analysis, the first thing to come to mind if the subject of financial charts comes up would probably be a chart pattern. Such formations as head and shoulders, flags, and triangles have eased their way into the non-technical vernacular.

Besides these Western chart patterns, many of those who are unfamiliar with technical analysis have also heard of such exotic candle patterns as doji, hammer, and hanging man. Because of the colorful nature of these names and their ability to convey a concise visual meaning, chart patterns have captured the imagination of countless investors who otherwise would not have delved into the field of technical analysis.

This chapter covers the two key areas of chart patterns: Western bar shapes and Japanese candlestick patterns. Both are vital to any trader's understanding of how technical analysis works, and both can be used to significant effect in making important trading decisions. This discussion begins with Western bar shapes.

Bar shapes are referred to here as "Western" only to help differentiate them from the Japanese candlestick patterns that have become so prevalent in recent years. Bar chart patterns have long been used in Western financial markets to classify price action and to help forecast probable price behavior. Each chart pattern carries its own theories, probabilities, and targets. Some are considered patterns that most often help a trend continue, while others are considered patterns that most often reverse a trend. However, these generalizations are not always entirely helpful, as traditional continuation patterns very often reverse a trend and traditional reversal patterns very often continue a trend. But for the purposes of classification, these patterns are described here according to the continuation/reversal convention. The one unifying theme of all Western bar chart patterns is that nothing happens until a break of the pattern is made. Bar patterns, as we shall soon see, are inevitably made to be broken.

Continuation Bar Patterns

The primary continuation patterns are triangles, flags, pennants, rectangles, and wedges. Of course, there are others that may be either more complex or less prevalent, but these are the primary continuation patterns that can be found on charts representing any financial market. To simplify even further, pennants may even be considered a type of triangle.

To begin with, the triangle pattern is perhaps the most prevalent continuation pattern on any chart. Triangles represent a converging consolidation, where the price bars are bordered by lines that come progressively closer to each other, ultimately to converge at a triangle apex. Ideally, price should break out of the triangle well before the apex is reached. The direction of the break is often in the direction of the trend preceding the triangle, making the formation what many consider to be a continuation pattern, but this is not always the case. Often price will break out in the opposite direction, making the triangle a reversal pattern. In any event, the direction of the price break is of less concern than the nature of the break. Pattern breaks with strong momentum are valued because of their higher probability of follow-through in the direction of the break. Conversely, many pattern breaks result in either a consolidation around the point of break or a false break scenario. Clearly, these types of pattern breaks are the bane of most chart pattern traders.

Three primary classifications of triangles comprise all of the triangles found on financial charts: symmetrical, ascending, and descending. Contrary to their label, symmetrical triangles do not actually need to be symmetrical. The only requirement of a symmetrical triangle, as shown in Exhibit 8.1, is that the upper border needs to be sloped downward while the lower border needs to be sloped upward. The angles of the slopes do not have to be equal. A symmetrical triangle represents a type of market equilibrium, or even indecision, that is manifested in a progressively tighter price consolidation.

In contrast to symmetrical triangles, ascending and descending triangles both have one border that is horizontal, or at least very close to horizontal. As shown in Exhibit 8.1, an ascending triangle is

EXHIBIT 8.1

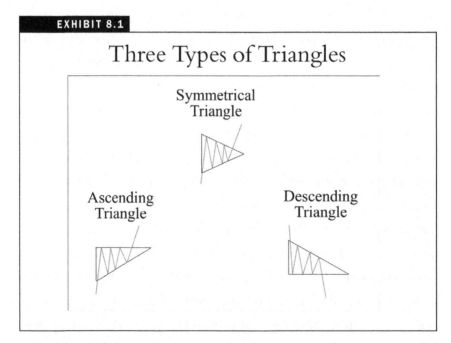

Three Types of Triangles

Symmetrical
Triangle

Ascending
Triangle

Descending
Triangle

Source: FX Solutions—FX AccuCharts

comprised of a horizontal top border with a lower border that is sloped upward. Like symmetrical triangles, ascending triangles represent a type of market equilibrium, but with some additional upside pressure. This is because the ascending triangle consolidation has a bottom border that is essentially a rising support trend line, while the top is static. As such, this type of triangle generally has somewhat of a bias to the upside when considering the direction of any subsequent break, but this is not always the case. Price may often break down below an ascending triangle.

Descending triangles, also shown in Exhibit 8.1, are comprised of a horizontal bottom border with an upper border that is sloped downward. Also like symmetrical triangles, descending triangles represent a type of market equilibrium, but with some additional downside pressure. This is because the descending triangle consolidation has a top border that is essentially a falling resistance trend line, while the bottom is static. As such, in an opposite fashion from an ascending triangle, a descending triangle generally has somewhat of a bias to the downside when considering the direction of any subsequent break. As with ascending triangles, however, this is not always the case. Price will often break out above a descending triangle.

Whichever type of triangle pattern is present, the consolidation theoretically should resolve itself by breaking out strongly in one direction, preferably in the direction of the prior trend, thereby shattering the delicate equilibrium. Of course, if price breaks out in the opposite direction, it can also be traded. As long as a bona fide break of any triangle occurs, in either direction, it can be viewed as a significant, potentially tradable event.

Whichever type of triangle appears, their approximate projected price targets are similarly derived. One would measure the triangle at its greatest height and then project that measure above the point of breakout (for up-moves) or below the point of breakout (for down-moves) to derive a potential target for the move.

Perhaps more than any other chart shape commonly labeled as a continuation pattern, flags and pennants most often fulfill the role in which they are categorized. In fact, the prior trend move is built into both of these patterns in the form of the flagpole. The expectation in a majority of flags and pennants is that a trend continuation is likely.

As shown in Exhibit 8.2, flag patterns are formed much like the flags in the noncharting world. As mentioned, there is a flagpole and

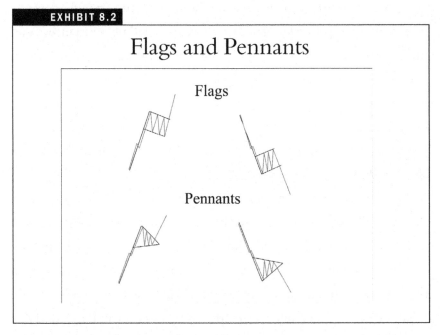

Flags and Pennants

Flags

Pennants

Source: FX Solutions—FX AccuCharts

then two parallel lines branching off the flagpole to represent the main flag consolidation. Ideal bullish flags have a strong upward-moving flagpole followed by a slightly downward-consolidating flag. Conversely, ideal bearish flags have a strong downward-moving flag-pole followed by a slightly upward-consolidating flag. When price action creates a flag pattern, the indication is that there is a strong directional move followed by a small, slightly countertrend retrace-ment or consolidation. The expectation after breaking out of this retracement/consolidation is that price is likely to continue the sharp trend in the direction of the flagpole.

The projected target of the subsequent move is equal to the point of breakout plus the vertical height of the flagpole (for up-moves), or the point of breakout minus the vertical height of the flagpole (for down-moves).

Having similarities with both flags and triangles, a pennant pat-tern may be best described as a small triangle (or wedge) on top of a flagpole. An even simpler, and perhaps more fitting, description of the pennant pattern is that it looks almost exactly like a real-life pennant. The triangle aspect of a pennant is usually smaller than a customary triangle pattern, but it does not have to be. Triangles are usually larger formations than flags or pennants, but again, this is more of an observation than a rule.

As shown in Exhibit 8.2, a pennant is composed of a flagpole followed by a small converging consolidation that looks like a small triangle (or a wedge). Bullish pennants have a flagpole that moves upward sharply, followed by the triangle consolidation. Conversely, bearish pennants have a flagpole that moves downward sharply, fol-lowed by the triangle consolidation. Like flags, when price action creates a pennant pattern, the indication is that there is a strong directional move followed by a small consolidation that is often somewhat counter to the trend. The expectation after breaking out of this consolidation is that price is likely to continue the sharp trend in the direction of the flagpole.

As with flags, the projected target of the subsequent move on a pennant break is equal to the point of breakout plus the vertical height of the flagpole (for up-moves) or the point of breakout minus the vertical height of the flagpole (for down-moves).

Like triangles, flags, and pennants, rectangles are also very common chart patterns. These patterns, as shown in Exhibit 8.3, are tight, horizontal consolidations with parallel upper and lower borders

EXHIBIT 8.3

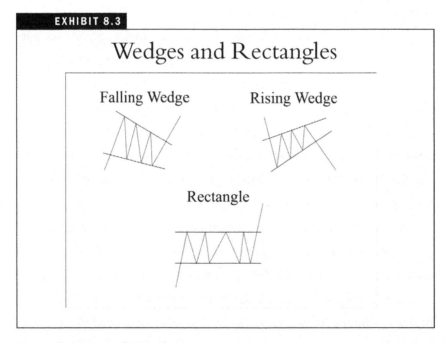

Wedges and Rectangles

Falling Wedge   Rising Wedge

Rectangle

Source: FX Solutions—FX AccuCharts

(resistance and support) that do not converge as triangles do. Rectangles are also sometimes called trading ranges. But while rectangles and trading ranges are both sideways consolidations bordered by parallel horizontal lines, there is a crucial difference in the way they are customarily traded. A trading range is usually a wider (or taller) consolidation that may be traded by some traders between its borders (i.e., long at the bottom of the range and short at the top of the range). In contrast, a rectangle is usually a tighter consolidation where traders will look to trade the breakout outside of the pattern, much as one would treat a triangle formation.

Also like triangles, rectangles represent market equilibrium and are often considered a rest in the midst of a trend move. For example, in an uptrend situation, a rectangle may appear as the bulls take a rest to regroup and prepare for a further onslaught.

As with triangles, however, this is not always the case. Rectangles can very well serve as reversal patterns. Most important, whichever direction the market decides to break, the nature of that break is vital. A clean and strong break is invariably more valuable than one that is hesitant.

Finding a projected target for a breakout of a rectangle pattern is simpler and more straightforward than for any other chart pattern. For an upward breakout, the price target would be derived simply by adding the height of the rectangle to the point of breakout. For a downward breakdown, the price target would be derived by subtracting the height of the rectangle from the point of breakdown. As with projected targets for all chart patterns, however, these should be considered more as general guidelines rather than precise projections.

Very similar to triangles, wedges are another chart pattern characterized by two converging lines. Unlike triangles, however, the two sides of a wedge slope in the same direction. Therefore, a rising wedge has two sides that both slope up, while a falling wedge has two sides that both slope down. See Exhibit 8.3 for examples.

Wedges represent market consolidation, much like other continuation patterns. But they also often represent countertrend retracement, even more so than triangles. As such, falling wedges that are continuation patterns ideally occur after up-moves, and will often be broken in the direction of the up-move. Likewise, rising wedges that are continuation patterns ideally occur after down-moves and will often be broken in the direction of the down-move.

There is no concrete targeting methodology for wedges, as there is for other chart patterns, but a break of a wedge pattern can be a strong catalyst for a major directional price move. As mentioned earlier in this chapter, a pennant is composed of a flagpole connected either to a triangle or a wedge. If a wedge is involved, it generally represents a greater countertrend retracement than a triangle.

TIPS AND TECHNIQUES

Volatility

The concept of volatility plays a vital role in technical analysis, especially in the subrealm of trend analysis. Many technical traders consider volatility carefully when making trading decisions. Marked changes in volatility are the main concern of these traders. To narrow it down even further, it is really the change in volatility from low to high, rather than vice versa, that is of the utmost interest.

Trending conditions are most often characterized by alternating periods of low and high volatility. Low volatility is usually considered price consolidation, equilibrium, or simply sideways price action. High volatility, in contrast, is often strongly directional, although this does not have to be the case. The shift from low volatility to high volatility is often manifested as a range expansion that marks the beginning or continuation of a trend. Therefore, this type of shift is vitally important to trend traders.

Every trend will generally go through alternating periods of rest and resumption during its life cycle. The "rest" portion (low volatility) could either be in the form of a sideways consolidation or a countertrend retracement. The "resumption" portion (shift to high volatility) is often in the form of a strong directional move. One of the most advantageous locations at which to enter a trend is when a period of rest suddenly becomes a period of resumption. This can be characterized as a volatility breakout, where low volatility shifts into high volatility, in the direction of the prevailing trend.

Continuation chart patterns like triangles, flags, pennants, and rectangles are simply diminished and/or diminishing areas of volatility that are just waiting for breakouts to higher volatility, most often in the direction of the trend. Besides these chart patterns, other methods of utilizing volatility shifts, or breakouts, include breaks of horizontal trading ranges, breaks of x-period highs or lows, and the Bollinger Bands "squeeze." These will be discussed in more detail later. Common technical tools for measuring volatility, as well as changes in volatility, are the average true range (ATR), Bollinger Bands, and the Bollinger BandWidth indicator.

Measuring and taking into consideration changes in volatility can be a vital component of making wise trading decisions, as volatility changes can give important clues as to the momentum of a market.

Reversal Bar Patterns

Whereas Western continuation patterns like triangles, flags, pennants, rectangles, and wedges are generally considered to continue a trend more often than not, Western reversal patterns are generally considered to reverse a trend more often than not.

As a side note, Japanese candlestick patterns, which will be discussed later in this chapter, excel at providing reversal indications, or confirmations. Arguably, the strongest Japanese candlestick patterns are those that hint at potential reversals. In contrast, Western bar chart patterns are perhaps better at providing trend continuation indications, with exceptionally prominent patterns like triangles, wedges, rectangles, and flags/pennants. At the same time, however, the three reversal bar patterns that will be discussed here have all shown their reliability over time. They are the double top/bottom, the triple top/ bottom, and the head and shoulders.

Each of these three patterns should ideally follow prolonged trends in order to fulfill its role as a true reversal pattern.

As shown in Exhibit 8.4, the double top/bottom is considered a classic reversal formation. As its name implies, a double top occurs when price hits the same or similar high twice consecutively after a major uptrend. Very importantly, the second top is considered a price failure since it was unable to make a significantly higher high above the first top. A major price failure is a good indication of weakening trend momentum and a possible impending reversal. The two peaks are separated by a trough. The signal to sell short comes on a subsequent breakdown below the lowest point in the trough. For targeting purposes, the vertical measure from the double

EXHIBIT 8.4

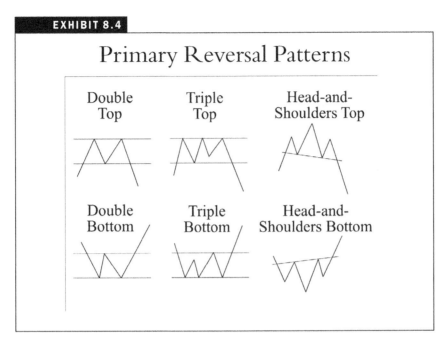

Source: FX Solutions—FX AccuCharts

top high down to the lowest point in the trough should be sub-tracted from the key point of breakdown (which is the lowest point in the trough).

A double bottom occurs when price hits the same or similar low twice consecutively after a major downtrend. The second bottom is considered a price failure. The two troughs are separated by a peak. The signal to buy comes on a subsequent breakout above the highest point in the peak. Much like with a double top, a double bottom target is derived by taking the vertical measure from the double bottom low up to the highest point in the peak and then adding that to the key point of breakout (which is the highest point in the peak).

As shown in Exhibit 8.4, the triple top/bottom is also considered a classic reversal formation. The triple top occurs when price hits the same or similar price high three times consecutively after a major uptrend. This pattern can be considered stronger than a double top because the failure of price to reach higher than the first peak occurs two times rather than just once. The three peaks are separated by troughs, of which there are a total of two that do not need to be at the same price level. The signal to sell short comes on a subsequent breakdown below the lowest of the two troughs. For targeting purposes, the vertical measure from the triple top high down to the lowest point in the lowest of the two troughs should be subtracted from the key point of breakdown (which is the lowest point in the lowest of the two troughs).

A triple bottom occurs when price hits the same or similar low three times consecutively after a major downtrend. The second and third bottoms are considered price failures, where price failed to move lower and to continue the downtrend. The three troughs are separated by peaks, of which there are a total of two that do not need to be at the same price level. The signal to buy comes on a subsequent breakout above the higher of the two peaks. For targeting purposes, the vertical measure from the triple bottom low up to the highest point in the highest of the two peaks should be added to the key point of breakout (which is the highest point in the highest of the two peaks).

Similar to the triple top/bottom, as shown in Exhibit 8.4, the head-and-shoulders pattern is perhaps the best-known chart pattern, or even the best-known single aspect of technical analysis, for the average layperson. Although it is not an extremely common pattern in most financial markets, its very visual name has captured the imaginations of traders and nontraders alike. The primary difference between the head-and-shoulders pattern and the triple top/bottom pattern lies in the middle of the pattern. For example, in a head-and-shoulders top, the middle peak (the head) is higher than both the left and right peaks (the shoulders). Conversely, in an inverted head-and-shoulders bottom, the middle trough (the head) is lower than both the left and right troughs (the shoulders).

The line connecting the troughs in a head-and-shoulders top, or the peaks in a head-and-shoulders bottom, is called the neckline. Breaks of the neckline are considered trading signals. In terms of a projected target, the vertical distance between the very top of the head to the neckline in a head-and-shoulders top is projected vertically down from the point of break (the neckline) to determine the price target. For a head-and-shoulders bottom, the vertical distance between the very bottom of the head to the neckline is projected vertically up from the point of break (again, the neckline) to determine the price target.

A head-and-shoulders reversal pattern, like the triple top/bottom pattern, represents a repeated attempt to continue the trend but an ultimate failure after multiple tries. The head within the pattern represents a false break in the direction of the trend and a resulting failure to follow through. After a third try (the right shoulder) that is unable even to reach the distance of the second (the head), failure is reinforced even further. A reversal is then confirmed if and when a neckline break occurs. Head-and-shoulders patterns are hard to miss on a chart. When they appear, they are usually large and prominent, screaming to be recognized. If a neckline break occurs on a head-and-shoulders pattern, the likelihood of follow-through on the reversal is significant. Head-and-shoulders formations that fail to complete as reversal patterns, however, are also prevalent.

Gaps

A chart pattern that can be considered either a continuation pattern or a reversal pattern, depending on the type and context, is a special category of pattern called a gap (an example of which is shown in Exhibit 8.5). These occur frequently in many financial markets

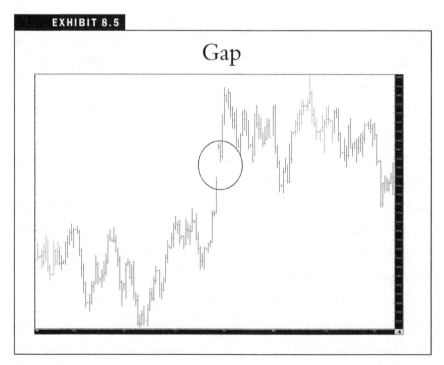

EXHIBIT 8.5

Gap

Source: FX Solutions—FX AccuCharts

when price makes a jump from one level to a separate, nonconsecutive level without visiting any prices in between the two levels. This empty separation means that no trading occurs at any price level within the gap. There can be a number of causes for gaps to occur, many of which are related to a faster-than-normal market due to new market information. This new information could be a news release, a substantial market-moving event, or an announcement that results in higher-than-normal market activity. Gaps occur frequently when a market first opens for the day or for the week, as new information that comes out while a market is closed can result in a price jump on market opening. A notable exception to this is the spot foreign exchange (forex) market, where gaps rarely occur. This is due to the fact that forex is the most liquid market in the world and runs continuously on a 24-hour basis (with the exception of weekends).

Several types of gaps are commonly found in many financial markets. These include common gaps, breakaway gaps, runaway gaps, and exhaustion gaps. Additionally, an island reversal pattern consists of two separate gaps. All of these primary gap patterns will be discussed here.

Common gaps are ones that occur frequently during normal market activity. These gaps have a relatively routine occurrence and are not usually caused by any major news or information. Because of this, common gaps carry less trading significance than the other types. Common gaps often get "filled" rather soon after they occur.

In contrast, breakaway gaps carry much more significance. This type of gap often follows periods of price consolidation when price is traversing a directionless, horizontal trading range. Breakaway gaps can often signify the beginning of a new trend and are thus much less likely than common gaps to be filled. In a new trend, momentum in the direction of the consolidation break is strengthened considerably by the occurrence of a breakaway gap. Confirmation on breakaway gaps can be derived from viewing trading volume. A gap that occurs on higher volume has a greater chance of succeeding as a breakaway gap and as a catalyst for a new trend.

Like breakaway gaps, runaway gaps carry substantial trend significance. In contrast to the trend-starting breakaway variety, however, runaway gaps occur somewhere in the middle of existing trends. Whereas a breakaway gap is preceded by sideways consolidation and followed by trending price action, a runaway gap is both preceded and followed by trending price action. When successful, this type of gap serves as a continuation pattern, signifying a continuation of the prevailing trend.

Exhaustion gaps, in contrast to the breakaway and runaway continuation gaps, are considered reversal patterns. An exhaustion gap can often be found when a trend's momentum literally exhausts itself. Therefore, this type of gap signifies that the trend is potentially on its last legs and may quickly either reverse or move into consolidation. Confirmation on exhaustion gaps can be derived from volume. As with breakaway gaps, an exhaustion gap that occurs on higher volume has a greater chance of succeeding as a true exhaustion gap and as a catalyst for a potential reversal. Because exhaustion gaps are reversal patterns, they are generally filled if and when the reversal actually occurs.

As mentioned earlier, island reversals consist of two gaps. These chart patterns are, as the name suggests, reversal patterns that form an island of consolidation between two price gaps. The first gap can be considered an exhaustion gap, while the second one can be considered a breakaway gap in the opposite direction. In an island-reversal-topping pattern, for example, price ends its previously prevailing uptrend with an exhaustion gap to the upside. After this gap up, a sideways price consolidation in the form of the "island" materializes. At the end of this island consolidation, a breakaway gap to the downside appears, after which price should continue down after the reversal to form a new downtrend. In an island-reversal-bottoming pattern, price ends its previously prevailing downtrend with an exhaustion gap to the downside. After this gap down, a sideways price consolidation in the form of the "island" materializes. At the end of this island consolidation, a breakaway gap to the upside appears, after which price should continue up after the reversal to form a new uptrend.

As a side note, Japanese candlestick patterns, which will be discussed next, refer to gaps as windows. There are rising windows (bullish gaps) and falling windows (bearish gaps). Instead of gaps being "filled," candlestick windows are "closed." In the candlestick world, windows are generally considered continuation signals. Since the concept of gaps has already been discussed in this section, the equivalent subject of windows will not be covered in the next section on Japanese candlestick patterns.

Gap patterns and combinations of gaps are important chart elements. Whether they are classified as reversal patterns or continuation patterns, depending on their nature and location, gaps can give traders and investors vital clues as to the momentum of a particular market.

Candlestick Patterns

With the primary Western bar patterns described, it is now time to turn to another kind of chart pattern that can give valuable clues to market price action: Japanese candlestick patterns.

As mentioned in Chapter 4, Japanese candlesticks and their patterns were introduced to the West by a pioneering trader by the name of Steve Nison, who brought this ancient charting method to America from its humble rice trading roots in Japan.

One of the primary differences between Western bars and Japanese candlesticks lies in the imaginative interpretation of candle patterns, which are labeled with equally imaginative names. Most candlestick patterns are considered either price reversal formations or patterns indicating indecision, while only a few are considered trend continuation formations. The primary value of candlesticks is that they visually depict the struggle between the market bulls (market participants who are looking for price to go up) and the market bears (market participants who are looking for price to go down).

Before moving onto a presentation of the most common and important candlestick patterns developed in Japan, it should be noted that these patterns were never meant to comprise a complete trading system. Rather, most high-level practitioners of candlestick analysis, including Steve Nison himself, readily state that candle patterns are intended either to confirm or be confirmed by other technical studies. Candle patterns should not be relied on exclusively to provide the full technical picture. That being said, however, candle patterns can contribute a tremendous amount of insight to any market technician's analytical process.

While the full repertoire of candlestick patterns includes many rare and exotic life-forms, a handful of the most common patterns comprise the bulk of price action in the major financial markets. As in other areas of technical analysis, as well as in most of life's endeavors, mastering the intricacies of the most important and prevalent candlestick patterns may prove to be more productive than attempting to obtain useful and lasting knowledge of all the patterns known to exist.

Therefore, a discussion, with illustrations, of the most prevalent and recognizable Japanese candlestick patterns found on financial price charts follows. Understanding and utilizing these alone can contribute a great deal to any trader's or investor's understanding of the struggle between market bulls and bears.

Single-Candle Patterns

Exhibit 8.6 provides a simple illustration of the most common single-candle patterns found in all major financial markets. A discussion of multiple-candle patterns follows.

As described in Chapter 4, a candle is composed of two primary components: the real body and the shadows. The real body is the thick part of the candle that represents the prices between the open and close of a given time period. If price closed above where it opened (a bullish candle) in that given time period, the body is a certain color (either white or green, depending on the specific charting software). In contrast, if price closed below where it opened (a bearish candle) in that given time period, the body is a different color (either black or red, depending on the specific charting software).

111

EXHIBIT 8.6

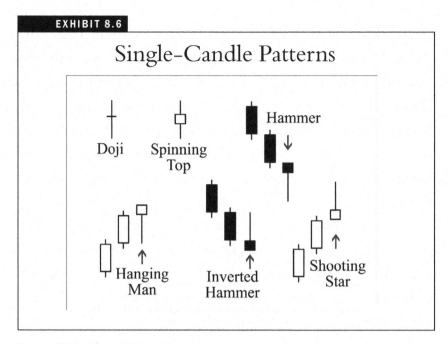

Single-Candle Patterns

Source: FX Solutions—FX AccuCharts

The shadows, or wicks, are thin, vertical lines that protrude above and below the real body. These shadows represent the highs and lows that price reached in the given time period.

Of all candlestick patterns, perhaps the doji is the simplest of all. Representing supreme indecision in the market, a doji is formed when a candle's open and close are either equal or very close to equal. After the doji opens, price may go up and/or down substantially, creating candle shadows in the process, but should close at or very near the open price. Again, this pattern represents indecision, or a tug-of-war, between buyers (bulls) and sellers (bears). With additional technical confirmation, a doji can often be considered a trend reversal indication.

Another sign of indecision similar to the doji is the spinning top. A spinning top has a very small real body (though not as small as the single line of a doji) with upper and lower shadows that are longer than the vertical length of the real body. With additional technical confirmation, spinning tops can also indicate potential trend reversals.

The primary message of both a spinning top and a doji is that price closes the trading period (candle) at or around the same price at which it opened. In between the open and close, price may have moved significantly in either direction, or both directions. This signifies that the market is undecided as to which direction to take. It can also signify the potential neutralizing of any previous trend that might have been in place, as countertrend forces may be slowing down, or even halting, the progress of trend forces in a hotly contested tug-of-war.

Hammers can be strong confirming indicators of potential trend reversals to the upside. A hammer candle occurs after a downtrend. Its appearance is top-heavy with the real body (the real body can be either color, bullish or bearish) and, very importantly, has a long lower shadow. This long lower shadow is the most important aspect of this candle, as it signifies that the previously prevailing bears attempted to push price lower but failed. While failures of this nature can often be the catalyst for reversing a downtrend, a hammer candle pattern, like other candle patterns, should only be used as a confirmation tool, and not as a sole or primary decision tool.

What a hammer candle is to a downtrend, a shooting star candle is to an uptrend. Essentially the opposite of a hammer, a shooting star is bottom-heavy with the real body and has a long upper shadow. The color of the real body (whether bullish or bearish) is unimportant. Shooting stars need to follow uptrends, much like hammers follow downtrends, and indicate confirmations of potential uptrend reversals. The long upper shadow of a shooting star is the most important aspect of the pattern, as it signifies that the previously prevailing bulls attempted to push price higher but failed. Much like the case with hammers, while failures of this nature can often be the catalyst for reversing an uptrend, a shooting star candle pattern should only be used as a confirmation tool, not as a sole or primary decision tool.

IN THE REAL WORLD

Pin Bars (Hammers and Shooting Stars)

Pin bars are essentially the equivalent of hammers and shooting stars in the candlestick world. These single-bar price action indicators can be exceptionally effective confirming factors for potential market turns. Used in conjunction with other trade decision factors, most notably support and resistance, pin bars can give valuable hints of market directional bias.

The basic concept of a bullish pin bar, or a hammer candle, is a long protruding bar pointing down, with the period open and close very close to each other near the top of the bar. These occur after bearish price runs. The basic concept of a bearish pin bar, or a shooting star candle, is a long protruding bar pointing up, with the period open and close very close to each other near the bottom of the bar. These occur after bullish price runs. Not only is the shape of pin bars important; the placement is also crucial. In order to be effective, these bars should follow well-defined directional runs.

After a defined bearish run, a bullish pin bar (hammer) that occurs right around an established support level is a good potential reversal confirmation. Similarly, after a defined bullish run, a bearish pin bar (shooting star) that occurs right around an established resistance level is also a good potential reversal confirmation.

Pin bars, or hammers and shooting stars, represent a potential exhaustion in previous momentum as well as a potential triumph of bulls over bears (for hammers) or bears over bulls (for shooting stars).

A hanging man candle looks identical to the appearance of a hammer candle but occurs after an uptrend instead of a downtrend. Just like the hammer, a hanging man is top-heavy with the real body and has a long lower shadow. The color of the real body is also irrelevant. As a hanging man should follow an uptrend, it can be considered a confirmation of a potential uptrend reversal. Its signal, however, arguably carries less weight than a hammer or a shooting star in its ability to signify a reversal confirmation, as a hanging man opens and closes near the top of its range after an uptrend. Therefore, the element of failure is not nearly as strong as with hammers and shooting stars.

Similarly, an inverted hammer looks identical to the appearance of a shooting star candle but occurs after a downtrend instead of an uptrend. Just like the shooting star, a hanging man is bottom-heavy with the real body and has a long upper shadow. The color of the real body is also irrelevant. As an inverted hammer should follow a downtrend, it can be considered a confirmation of a potential downtrend reversal. Like the hanging man, however, its signal arguably carries less weight than a hammer or a shooting star in its ability to signify a reversal confirmation, as an inverted hammer opens and closes near the bottom of its range after a downtrend. Therefore, as with hanging man patterns, the element of failure in inverted hammers is not nearly as strong as with hammers and shooting stars.

Multiple-Candle Patterns

In contrast to the primary single-candle patterns just described, multiple-candle patterns are comprised of more than one candle. Exhibit 8.7 provides a simple illustration of the most common multiple-candle patterns found in all major financial markets.

EXHIBIT 8.7

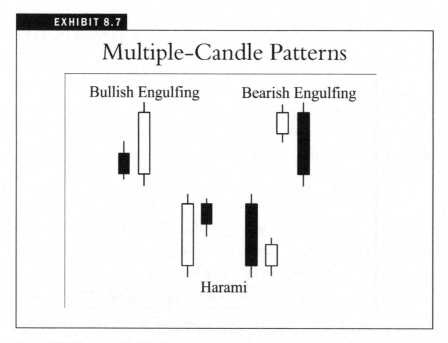

Multiple-Candle Patterns

Bullish Engulfing   Bearish Engulfing

Harami

Source: FX Solutions—FX AccuCharts

The bullish engulfing pattern is a bullish reversal pattern that usually occurs after a downtrend. It is a two-candle pattern that is usually considered a reversal confirmation. The first candle has a small bearish real body, and the second candle has a large bullish real body that completely encompasses the first candle's real body range. The concept behind this two-candle pattern is that the small body of the first candle represents hesitancy to continue a downtrend, while the large body of the second candle represents the bulls overpowering the previously prevailing bears, potentially reversing the downtrend.

In an opposite fashion, the bearish engulfing pattern is a bearish reversal pattern that usually occurs after an uptrend. It is also a two-candle pattern that is usually considered a reversal confirmation. The first candle has a small bullish real body, and the second candle has a large bearish real body that completely encompasses the first candle's real body range. The concept behind this two-candle pattern is that the small body of the first candle represents hesitancy to continue an uptrend, while the large body of the second candle represents the bears overpowering the previously prevailing bulls, potentially reversing the uptrend.

The opposite of an engulfing pattern is a harami pattern, a two-candle pattern that consists of a large body followed by a smaller, encompassed body of the opposite color. Therefore, a harami pattern can either be a large bullish candle followed by a small bearish candle or a large bearish candle followed by a small bullish candle. Like engulfing patterns, harami patterns are also considered potential reversal confirmations. Harami patterns represent indecision after strong trends, as is evidenced by the small body of the second candle in the pattern.

There are many other multiple-candle patterns in existence, but those described in this chapter comprise the most prevalent, and therefore the most potentially useful, patterns found on charts in every major financial market.

Both single-candle and multiple-candle patterns can contribute a great deal to any trader's or investor's understanding of market price action. Combined with Western chart patterns and other technical tools for analyzing financial markets, candle patterns are another important key to forming high-probability trading decisions.

One of these other technical tools is the moving average, a vital component of every market technician's toolbox. This is the subject of Chapter 9.

Summary

This chapter explored the realm of chart patterns—both Western bar shapes and Japanese candlestick patterns. Starting off with traditional Western continuation patterns like triangles, flags, pennants, rectangles, and wedges, the discussion progressed to Western reversal patterns like double tops/bottoms, triple tops/bottoms, and the well-known head-and-shoulders pattern. Then the several forms of gap patterns were covered, including common gaps, breakaway gaps, runaway gaps, exhaustion gaps, and, finally, two-gap island reversals.

The most prevalent Japanese candlestick patterns were then introduced, including single-candle patterns like doji, spinning tops, hammers, shooting stars, hanging men, and inverted hammers. Common multiple-candle patterns include engulfing patterns and harami.

CHAPTER 9

The World of Moving Averages

After reading this chapter, you will be able to:

- Know the basic definition, structure, and mathematical basis of a moving average.
- Identify the differences among the most common types of moving averages.
- Understand the many uses of moving averages in technical trading and analysis.
- Appreciate the advantages and disadvantages of using moving averages.

Introduction to Moving Averages

In the field of technical analysis, moving averages are the tool that many beginners first gravitate toward. This is due in part to the fact that these wavy lines are perhaps among the easiest elements to grasp,

EXHIBIT 9.1

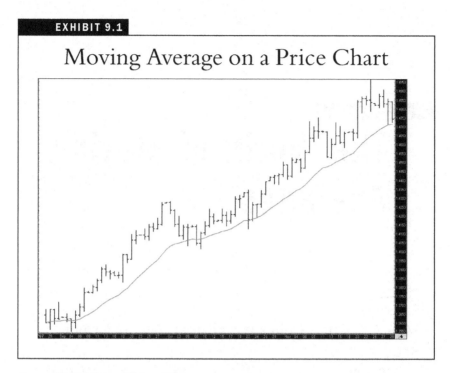

Moving Average on a Price Chart

Source: FX Solutions—FX AccuCharts

as well as among the simplest tools for both analyzing trends and building straightforward trading strategies.

As shown in Exhibit 9.1, a moving average is simply a line placed directly on a price chart that dynamically calculates the mean average of prices over a defined number of past periods. For each period, this calculated average price is plotted as a point on the price chart, and these points are connected to form a dynamically changing line that coexists with the price bars.

When plotted in this way on a financial price chart, the fluctuations in price are smoothed so that market noise is reduced, depending on the number of periods that are averaged, and the trend can be better revealed.

The primary variable when implementing a moving average is the look-back period. This simply equates to the number of preceding price periods (usually period closes) that are included in the calculation of the average. For example, on a daily chart where each bar or candle is worth 1 day of price action, a 20-period moving average will take the running average of the daily closing prices for the last 20 trading days. For another example, on a 5-minute chart where each bar or candle is worth 5 minutes of price action, a 200-period moving average will take the running average of the closing prices for the last 200 5-minute periods.

There are several different variations of moving averages, the most common of which are the simple moving average (SMA), the exponential moving average (EMA), and the weighted moving average (WMA). The differences among these three types of moving averages lie in their mathematical weighting of prices when deriving the averages. For the most part, the visual differences among the three types, as shown in Exhibit 9.2, are not drastic.

The main difference lies in the fact that SMAs assign equal weighting to all of the prices within the given number of look-back periods, while EMAs and WMAs assign greater mathematical weighting to more recent prices within the given number of look-back periods. EMAs and WMAs have differing mathematical constructs, but their concepts and philosophies are similar. Proponents of EMAs and WMAs argue that recent price action is more significant and has a greater impact on future direction than older price action. Therefore, they reason that more recent price action should be given a

EXHIBIT 9.2

Three Types of Moving Average Displayed on Price Chart

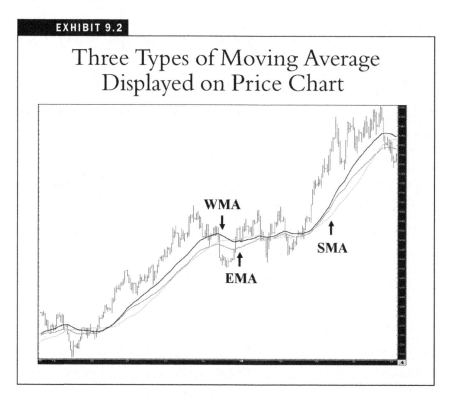

Source: FX Solutions—FX AccuCharts

greater weighting when deriving a moving average. EMAs and WMAs are generally more sensitive to recent price changes than SMAs. At the same time, however, the popularity of the SMA has not suffered, and it continues to enjoy substantial usage in all financial markets. Key SMAs, such as the 200–period and 50–period, are used by many traders and investors as price benchmarks and are often prominently displayed in the financial media as important technical indicators.

From an analytical big-picture perspective, moving averages are used to provide a clearer depiction of trend direction and strength than one might have by looking at price bars alone. Trend direction can often be deduced at a glance simply by looking to see if a moving average is traveling higher or lower on the price scale. Trend strength can be judged by the relative slope of a moving average—steeper for stronger trends and flatter for weaker trends. An exceptionally flat moving average can be considered an indication of no trend at all, which usually manifests itself as a sideways price consolidation that fails to make any significant progress in either direction.

Moving Average Crossovers

Besides serving as a trend indicator, moving averages are often utilized as key elements of trading strategies. The simplest of these strategies is the moving average crossover. There are several different variations of the moving average crossover, the most common of which will be discussed here.

The most basic crossover, as shown in Exhibit 9.3, involves the intersection of price and a single moving average. If price crosses above the moving average, it would represent a possible opportunity to buy. Conversely, if price crosses below the moving average, it would represent a possible opportunity to sell short. There are certain limitations to this simple type of moving average trading strategy, but these will be discussed later in this chapter.

The second type of crossover, as shown in Exhibit 9.4, is probably the most commonly used moving average strategy for beginning traders. It involves the use of two moving averages with different look-back period settings. If the shorter-period moving average crosses above the longer-period moving average, that would be

EXHIBIT 9.3

Crossovers of Price and One Moving Average

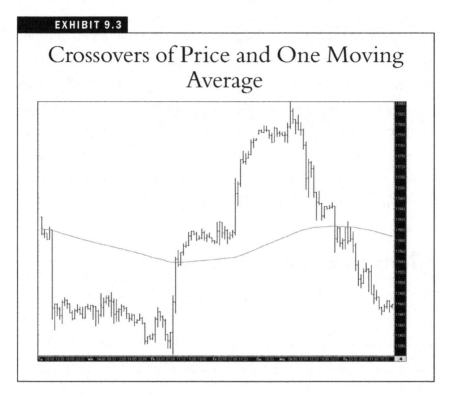

Source: FX Solutions—FX AccuCharts

considered a signal to buy. Conversely, if the shorter-period moving average crosses below the long-period moving average, that would be considered a signal to sell short. Certain limitations also affect this moving average trading strategy, but again, these will be discussed later in this chapter.

The third primary type of moving average crossover, as shown in Exhibit 9.5, involves the use of three moving averages. This method of using multiple confirming crossovers attempts to help combat some of the limitations inherent in moving average crossovers that were mentioned earlier, including the potentially unprofitable "whipsaw"

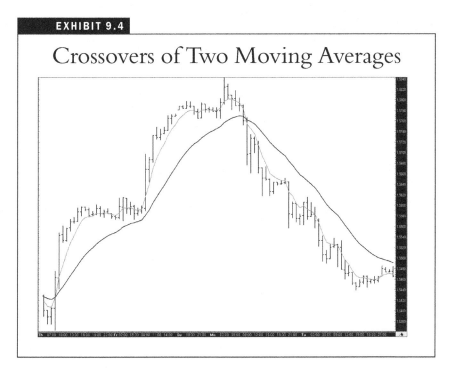

EXHIBIT 9.4

Crossovers of Two Moving Averages

Source: FX Solutions—FX AccuCharts

price action that often results from nontrending, sideways-moving markets. Trading strategies employing three different moving averages usually produce signals when the shortest of the moving averages crosses over the two longer moving averages, or when the shortest moving average crosses over the middle one and then the middle one crosses over the longest one. The idea is to require additional confirmation of directional momentum, as revealed by the multiple moving average crossovers, before a trade is fully committed to.

Generally, most trading systems that utilize moving averages are always in the market. That is, when a trade is opened on a crossover and then closed on an opposite crossover, another trade is

EXHIBIT 9.5

Crossovers of Three Moving Averages

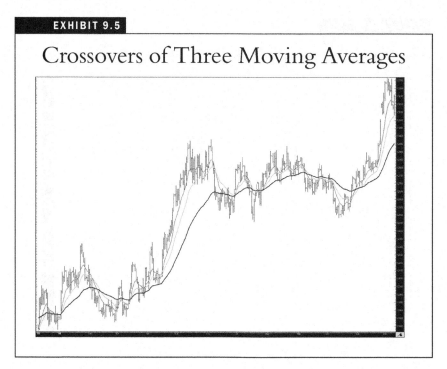

Source: FX Solutions—FX AccuCharts

immediately opened in the opposite direction to take the place of the previous trade. Therefore, there is always at least one trade open, whether long or short, depending on the prevailing crossover signal.

The objective of such moving average crossover trading strategies is to capture profits during prolonged market trending conditions. Losses suffered during those inevitable nontrending, sideways-moving markets are acceptable insofar as they can be overcome in the long run by generally larger trend profits. Therefore, for those using a moving average crossover system, taking every single cross-over trading signal becomes almost a necessity, lest the trader miss out on any highly sought-after trend trading opportunities.

The limitations of moving average crossover systems, as mentioned earlier, lie primarily in what occurs during nontrending markets. Sideways price action, as shown in Exhibit 9.6, manifests itself in moving averages as multiple crossovers in quick succession. Although crossover signals can often be exceptionally profitable during trending markets, traders or investors who are considering using them as their primary strategy should be forewarned that they must be prepared for frequent losses resulting from common whipsaw price action. Whipsaw can occur regardless of however many moving averages and confirmation crossovers happen to be utilized in a given trading system. Nontrending, sideways price action causes

EXHIBIT 9.6

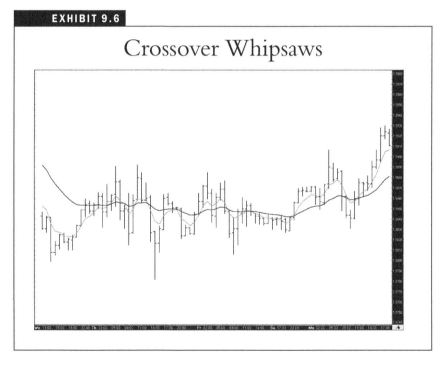

Crossover Whipsaws

Source: FX Solutions—FX AccuCharts

these whipsaws to occur, which results in excessive crossovers with little to no follow-through. These often lead to multiple small losses that can quickly erode the trading accounts of anyone following these signals faithfully.

Therefore, as mentioned earlier in this chapter, the only way to achieve net profitability with moving average crossovers, given the prevalence of whipsaws in all financial markets, is to take full advantage all true trending opportunities. This occurs when moving averages are separated substantially and crossovers are few and far between. If a trader can truly exploit these trending opportunities, the many times when sideways price action results in abundant crossover whipsaws and small losses can be both withstood and accepted.

 **TIPS AND TECHNIQUES**

Correct Order of Multiple Moving Averages

There are many methods for determining the existence, strength, and direction of a trend. These methods include trend lines, trend channels, linear regression, slopes of moving averages, the average directional index indicator, simple visual estimation, and more.

One effective method utilizing moving averages is the correct order of multiple moving averages. This is shown in Exhibit 9.7. An example of this technique involves the use of five different exponential moving averages, although more or fewer may be used according to any particular trader's desires. The periods of the moving averages may also be varied experimentally, but one example of a moving average combination uses these five EMA periods: 10, 20, 30, 50, and 100. Many traders have been known to choose periods based on Fibonacci numbers (e.g., 5, 13, 34, 55, and 89). Extensive experimentation with the quantity and periods of moving averages helps tremendously in identifying a good set of multiple moving averages that works well for the market being traded.

EXHIBIT 9.7

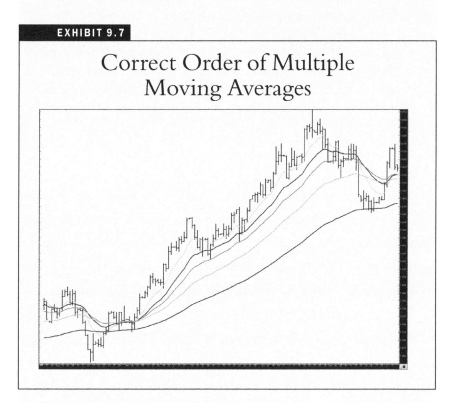

Correct Order of Multiple Moving Averages

Source: FX Solutions—FX AccuCharts

Once the quantity and periods are identified, trend determination with multiple moving averages simply consists of considering whether the EMAs are in the correct order at any

given time. If the longest-period EMA is on the bottom and progressively shorter-period EMAs are stacked above it, with the
shortest-period EMA on top, that can be considered the correct
order for an uptrend. If the shortest-period EMA is on the bottom
and progressively longer-period EMAs are stacked above it,
with the longest-period EMA on top, that can be considered the
correct order for a downtrend. Whether an uptrend or a downtrend is indicated, trend-following strategies can then be implemented to enter into trades in the direction of the prevailing
trend. Moving averages that are not in correct order indicate
that there is a lack of a directional trend. In this event, one might
be well advised to stay out of trading in that particular market at
that particular time, especially if one prefers to trade in the direction of the trend.

Besides the whipsaw inherent in trading moving average crossovers, a related weakness in moving averages lies in the fact that they
invariably lag, or follow, price. Moving averages, therefore, can never
be predictive, as price always arrives at its destination well before any
moving average could. Consequently, although moving averages can
certainly do a good job of describing a current trend, they are lacking
when it comes to signaling changes in trends. This is a major weakness that prevents moving averages from serving as reliable trend
change indicators. Partly in efforts to make moving averages more
sensitive to trend changes and price moves, and therefore to combat
the inherent lag, different calculations that stress more recent price
action (e.g., EMAs and WMAs) were introduced to provide an alter-
native to the less sensitive calculations of SMAs. As innovative and
different as the weighted calculations are, however, the lag in moving

averages is unavoidable, whichever variation of moving average is ultimately used. This is not at all to say, however, that lag renders moving averages unusable. Rather, the lag effect simply makes moving averages less effective at indicating trend changes and reversals than they are at describing trends in progress.

Moving Averages as Support and Resistance

Aside from its use as a trend direction and strength indicator as well as its prominence in the ubiquitous crossover strategies, the humble moving average is often also used in its capacity as a dynamic support and resistance indicator, much in a similar fashion as a trend line, but wavy and fluid instead of straight.

Because prices will often bounce consistently off certain EMAs when in trending mode, as shown in Exhibit 9.8, some traders will trade these bounces in the direction of the trend when markets appear to be entrenched in strong trending situations. This type of trading is very similar to trading with trend lines.

To go a step further, not only may moving averages be used to enter into trend trades using bounces off the line as entries, but these versatile tools can also be used to signal potential trade exits.

As shown in Exhibit 9.9, a 20-period EMA can be used to describe a strong trend, and will also often serve as a dynamic support line for an uptrend or a dynamic resistance line for a downtrend. When this occurs, traders can be relatively confident that a strong trend is indeed in place, at least for the time being. If a trader had gotten into this hypothetical trend using the moving average bounce entry, or really any entry method into a strongly trending market, a

EXHIBIT 9.8

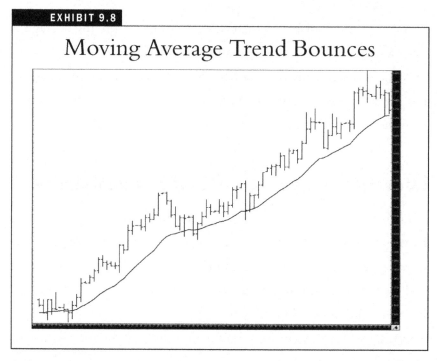

Moving Average Trend Bounces

Source: FX Solutions—FX AccuCharts

logical trade exit signal would occur when price violates and then closes a bar/candle on the other side of the moving average. This can be called a moving average break-and-close exit. The logic behind this is straightforward. If a moving average can act as a dynamic support or resistance level in a trending situation, where a bounce off the line can serve as a trade entry signal, it is only reasonable that if the line is violated on the other side (with a bar close for additional confirmation), a trade exit signal will have been produced. Exiting trades using moving averages in this manner often are among the most advantageous methods for taking profits after strong trend trades.

EXHIBIT 9.9

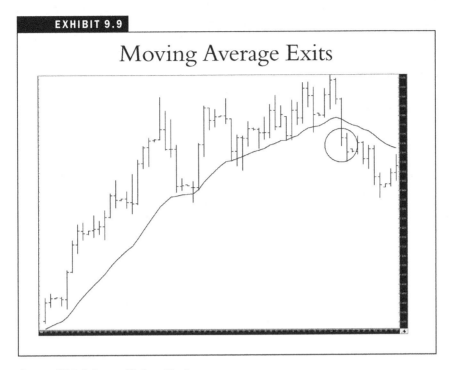

Moving Average Exits

Source: FX Solutions—FX AccuCharts

As discussed throughout this chapter, moving averages are extremely versatile tools that can be used to assess the direction and strength of any price trend, to capture and exploit trends using crossovers, and to provide opportunities both to enter and to exit trades using bounces off a moving average and violations of a moving average, respectively. These capabilities are substantial, despite the limitations moving averages have in terms of both lagging price action and producing frequent whipsaws during sideways, nontrending markets.

Besides moving averages, a whole host of other important indicators provide traders and investors with key technical information.

Many of the most popular and prevalent of these indicators will be the subject of Chapter 10.

Summary

This chapter introduced the world of moving averages, including the definition and structure of the most common types of moving averages: simple, exponential, and weighted. These key trend-following tools are often used to denote a market's trend direction and trend strength, and can be used in practical trading in the form of moving average crossovers. The phenomenon of whipsaw, where sideways price action results in multiple crossovers in quick succession, is one of the key drawbacks to using moving average crossovers during nontrending markets. Moving averages can also be used effectively as dynamically changing support and resistance trend lines, where trades can be initiated on bounces and exits can be executed on breaks.

CHAPTER 10

Key Technical Indicators and Oscillators

After reading this chapter, you will be able to:

- Become familiar with many of the most common indicators used by technical traders and analysts in all major financial markets.
- Appreciate how oscillators are a special subset of indicators that measure market momentum and price divergences.
- Understand how different indicators and oscillators are applied during different market conditions.

Introduction to Indicators and Oscillators

When many people think of technical analysis, aside from thinking of chart shapes and patterns, they think of indicators. Moving averages, as discussed in the last chapter, comprise a type of indicator. But many more play pivotal roles in technical trading.

Generally speaking, technical indicators are mathematically derived representations of price that purport to provide additional information above and beyond what price alone reveals. There are countless indicators in existence, most with their own unique calculations that package price action in a different, and often innovative, way. Some of these indicators are meant to be used for a specific financial market, such as equities or futures. Others can be used equally well on charts of all financial markets. This chapter covers only the latter—universal indicators that are nonspecific with regard to the market. Furthermore, only the most common and prominent of the extremely numerous indicators in existence are discussed here. There is a reason for the widespread usage of these common indicators, and they are therefore discussed here as among the essentials of technical analysis.

New indicators have proliferated throughout the years since the inception of chart reading. But what many discover, after extensive exploration of the many different available tools, is that the key indicators described here, ones that have withstood the test of time and have prevailed, are much more than sufficient to choose from.

IN THE REAL WORLD

Paralysis by Analysis

Paralysis by analysis is a very common affliction, especially among technical traders. It can occur when traders have too many studies or indicators on their charts and seek endless confirmations before taking any action. This is the polar opposite of traders who initiate trades recklessly based on gut feeling alone. Paralysis by analysis may be the lesser of the two evils, but both of these afflictions can be extremely detrimental to any trader.

There is a lot of good in being cautious and conservative when deciding to take trades, but becoming paralyzed by the decision-making process can be completely counterproductive. Having all of the many latest and greatest indicators on one's charts may look impressive to the uninitiated, but it will not help one to become a better or more successful trader. In fact, in many cases, indicator overload actually hinders one from attaining consistent trading success.

A good remedy against paralysis by analysis is a combination of solid risk control and optimal money management practices. Technical analysis can be very helpful in setting risk management measures, such as logically placed stop-losses that are neither too tight nor too loose, as well as well-formulated risk:reward ratios. Additionally, intelligent money management is an absolute essential for any trader who wants to be successful. With these measures in place, traders need not be paralyzed by the trade entry process. No trader will ever come anywhere even close to 100 percent correct, even in the unlikely event that 50 indicators, oscillators, and squiggly lines are all pointing in the same direction at the same time. But many traders can still be consistently successful, as long as risk controls and money management are in good order.

This is not at all to say that traders should ever just jump into trades without first doing proper analysis. As mentioned, this is also an extreme that should definitely be avoided. But many traders are utterly unable to pull the buy/sell trigger unless all of the many stars in the galaxy are perfectly aligned. This never happens.

The most prudent path is to stick to the essentials and use only the tools that prove to work the best over time. When a good opportunity presents itself according to careful analysis, that opportunity should be taken—provided that the proper risk controls and money management guidelines are in place.

Within the world of indicators, oscillators are a special subset. Their primary purpose is to give readings of momentum. This includes the ubiquitous extreme readings of "overbought" and "oversold." Oscillators usually "oscillate," as their name suggests, within a defined range, and so are often used by traders and investors to help define price turns and reversals within a horizontal range, as opposed to a trending market. Some of these oscillators can, however, be applied effectively during trends. This is discussed later in this chapter.

Before descriptions of each key indicator are presented, it is important to note that most indicators suffer the same inherent limitations that plague moving averages as well as any other derivative of price. That is, indicators that are mathematically derived from price are often considered simply to be lagging reflections of price. Many would argue that because of this lagging effect, indicators that simply follow price action cannot reveal anything more than price alone could reveal. These same people would argue that while indicators may be great at describing what price has done in the past, they would be hard-pressed to provide any reliable clues as to what might happen next. For this reason, indicators are often relegated to serving as secondary confirmation tools by traders who subscribe to this argument.

While it may be true that most indicators are simply a repackaged version of price itself, it is often exactly that kind of repackaging that is needed to illuminate high-probability trading opportunities. What some traders may fail to see on the price bars alone may be crystal clear to them on an indicator derived from price. In this same vein, many professional traders perform their chart analysis exclusively on a chosen indicator or oscillator (e.g., relative strength index or commodity channel index), often even to the complete exclusion of price bars. This type of trading is not quite mainstream, but it illustrates how vitally important indicators can be in technical analysis and trading. Even if indicators are not used as the primary analytical tool, they can still be extremely valuable in augmenting price action analysis.

Key Indicators

To begin a discussion of specific indicators, one of the most prominent and popular analysis tools available is derived from moving averages. It is called moving average convergence/divergence and

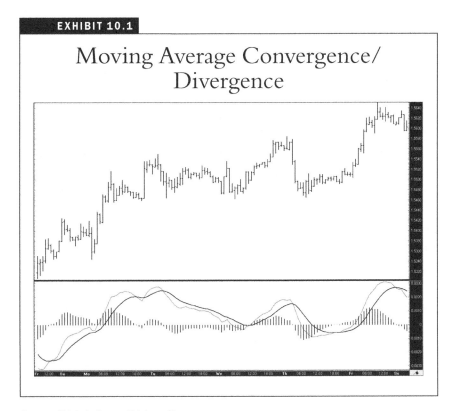

EXHIBIT 10.1

Moving Average Convergence/
Divergence

Source: FX Solutions—FX AccuCharts

is shown in Exhibit 10.1. Commonly referred to by its acronym, MACD, it was developed by a technical analyst named Gerald Appel. Since its introduction by Appel in the 1970s, the MACD has become one of the most prevalent indicators/oscillators ever invented. Many technical traders use MACD as their sole confirming indicator. Others take trading signals exclusively from the MACD. This multi-faceted indicator acts as a sign of trend momentum by representing the relationship between two moving averages. MACD can be traded by taking signals from crossovers of the two lines, crosses above or below the zero line, and price oscillator divergence, among other uses. There are three major components to the MACD indicator: the MACD line, the trigger line, and the histogram.

Developed by their namesake, John Bollinger, a well-known trader and portfolio manager, Bollinger Bands are generally over-laid directly on a chart's price bars/candles. As shown in Exhibit 10.2, the bands consist of a simple moving average (SMA) with two additional lines: one that is a certain number of standard deviations above the SMA and the other that is the same number of standard deviations below the SMA. By default, Bollinger Bands are usually set with a 20-period SMA along with two outer lines, each at 2 standard deviations away from the SMA, one above and the other below. But these settings can be readily changed to suit the trading environment. The primary purpose of the Bollin-ger Bands indicator is to measure a currency pair's volatility around the mean (which is represented by the SMA). The bands are often used to give indications of impending volatility increases (when the bands tighten). They can also be used to provide indi-cations of overbought or oversold market conditions.

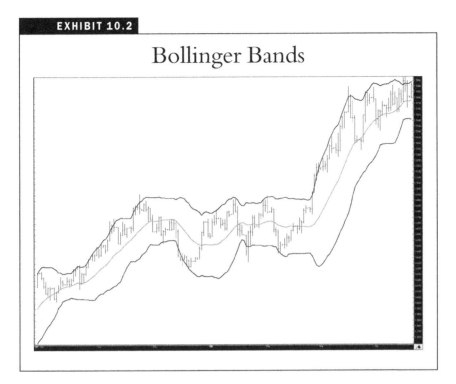

Bollinger Bands

Source: FX Solutions—FX AccuCharts

A well-known trading technique that utilizes the Bollinger Bands is called the *squeeze*. This method, as shown in Exhibit 10.3, exploits the well-observed tendency for periods of high volatility in financial markets to follow periods of low volatility. Low volatility on the Bollinger Bands is represented by a tightening, or a narrowing of the bands. This is the squeeze. The anticipated event after this period of low volatility is a sudden, sharp increase in volatility, which often manifests itself as a substantial directional move. Thus, traders may take advantage of this burst of volatility by jumping on a trade once price breaks away from the Bollinger Bands squeeze.

EXHIBIT 10.3

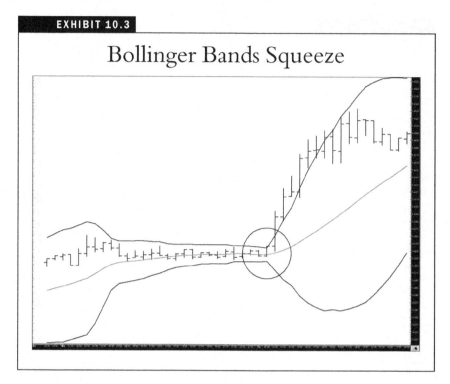

Bollinger Bands Squeeze

Source: FX Solutions—FX AccuCharts

The average directional index (ADX), as shown in Exhibit 10.4, was developed by a prolific developer of indicators, J. Welles Wilder. The ADX resides vertically either above or below the bar or candle price chart. The purpose of this indicator is to measure the strength, or lack of strength, of the current trend as well as whether the trend is increasing or decreasing in strength. Strong trends have high ADX readings, while nontrending markets have low ADX readings. An increasing ADX reading is a sign that the trend may be increasing in strength, while a decreasing ADX reading is a sign that the trend may be decreasing in strength or moving toward consolidation. Many traders who use ADX will place a horizontal line of demarcation on

EXHIBIT 10.4

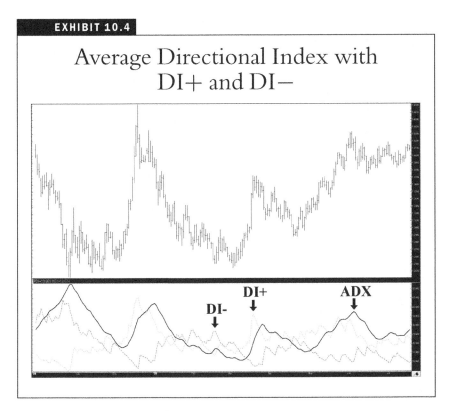

Average Directional Index with DI+ and DI−

Source: FX Solutions—FX AccuCharts

the indicator to mark the general boundary between trending and nontrending. A popular location to place this line is at the 30 level. Once this level is set, the trader may then institute a guideline that if the ADX moves above the 30 level, it is moving into strong trending mode. Conversely, if the ADX moves below the 30 level, it is approaching a nontrending, consolidating state. This is an important distinction that can help the trader determine when to use trend-trading techniques and when to turn to range-trading techniques.

It is important to note that ADX by itself does not provide any indication as to the direction of the trend. This function is fulfilled by two other indicators that are closely related to and frequently used with ADX: DI+ and DI− (as shown in Exhibit 10.4), where "DI" stands for directional indicator. These two indicators provide the directional component to the ADX. When DI+ is moving up and DI− is moving down, it means that price is bullish, or going up. When DI− is moving up and DI+ is moving down, it means that price is bearish, or going down. Some traders will look for crossovers of the DI+ and DI− to provide directional trading signals. ADX, in conjunction with DI+ and DI−, can give vital clues to aid in the important task of determining market trend strength.

Average true range (ATR) is another useful indicator introduced by J. Welles Wilder that also resides vertically either above or below a price chart. As shown in Exhibit 10.5, ATR is an average measure of recent price volatility. It is calculated as a moving average of a given span of past period ranges. For example, if one wishes to calculate, on an ongoing basis, the average daily price range for a security for the most recent 10 days, one would simply plot a 10-period ATR on a daily price chart of that security. This would produce each day a running average of the daily price ranges for the most recent 10-day period. As ATR is a key measure of recent market volatility, when the indicator has a high reading, recent volatility has been high. When a low reading is given, recent volatility has been low. Among other important uses, ATR is often used as the basis for setting logical stop-losses and price targets based on recent volatility in a given financial market.

The parabolic stop and reverse (SAR) is an indicator that excels at providing a sensible trailing stop and reverse methodology.

EXHIBIT 10.5

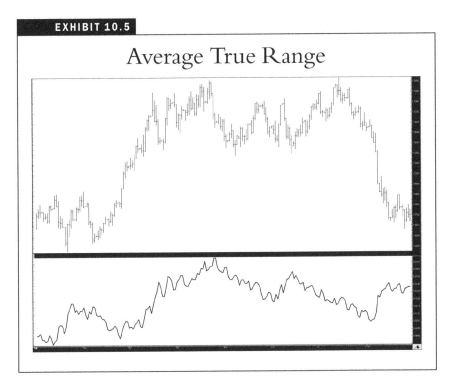

Average True Range

Source: FX Solutions—FX AccuCharts

Trailing stops are useful elements of an overall stop-loss and risk management strategy. This indicator is yet another that was originated by J. Welles Wilder in his pioneering work on chart indicators. As shown in Exhibit 10.6, the parabolic SAR is usually comprised of dots that follow price in such a way that if a dot is below a price bar, the trade should be long with a dynamic stop-loss at the dot. Conversely, if the dot is above the price bar, the trade should be short with a dynamic stop-loss at the dot. This indicator, therefore, provides the trader with a built-in trading system for being long or short, with the added bonus of convenient locations for stop-losses. Like many other indicators, however, the

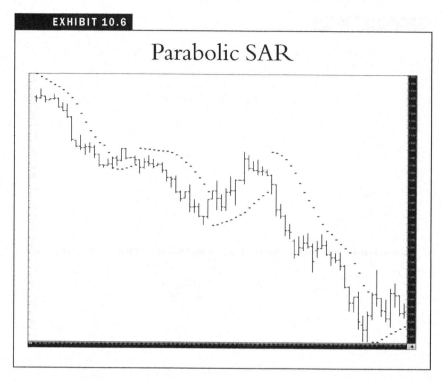

EXHIBIT 10.6

Parabolic SAR

Source: FX Solutions—FX AccuCharts

parabolic SAR can be prone to vicious whipsaws where the trading signals result in a string of losses due to the lack of a strong trend. But the fact that this indicator stresses a logical use of the trailing stop-loss concept makes it a valuable tool for any technical trader.

Another valuable indicator used by technical analysts and traders is the linear regression indicator, as shown in Exhibit 10.7. Linear regression trend lines use statistical principles to define trends in a market, without relying on human judgment bias. The basic principles behind linear regression include the statistical concepts of normal distribution, standard deviation, and reversion to the mean. Usually, a

EXHIBIT 10.7

Linear Regression Indicator

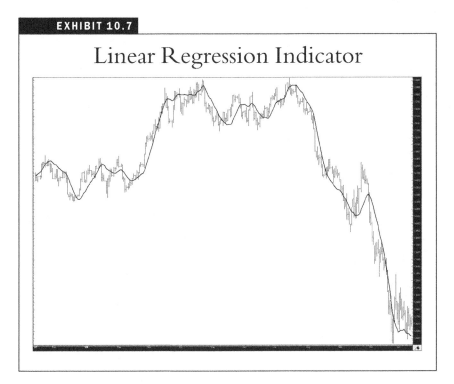

Source: FX Solutions—FX AccuCharts

linear regression line is drawn much like any common trend line, but through the middle area of prices rather than at the extremes. The central idea behind this is to identify times when price has deviated significantly from the mean and when it might potentially be reverting back to the mean once again. This creates possible trading opportunities on mean reversion price moves. The linear regression indicator differs from the linear regression line in that the indicator is not a straight line. Rather, it curves through price action. This is due to the fact that it connects the end points of all the straight linear regression trend lines, producing an automatic, dynamic plot of linear regression on a price chart.

Key Oscillators

As mentioned earlier, there is a special subset of indicators that are called oscillators. These indicators fulfill a special role in that they generally concentrate on market momentum and excel at providing readings of price overextension that are normally referred to as overbought and oversold.

As their name suggests, oscillators oscillate within a generally defined range, and so are often used by traders and investors to help define price turns and reversals within ranging markets. Within trending situations, however, oscillators can still serve a useful purpose, as discussed in this chapter.

Many oscillators are similar in their mathematical formulas as well as in their function and appearance. Therefore, using numerous oscillators on a single chart can be considered redundant in many cases. Only the most widely used and important oscillators are described here.

Generally, when an oscillator reading is above a certain overbought threshold during a trading range, the indication is that upward momentum may soon be exhausted and that an impending downward turn may potentially occur. On the other side, when an oscillator reading is below a certain oversold threshold during a trading range, the indication is that downward momentum may soon be exhausted and that an impending upward turn may occur.

Very importantly, another key function of chart oscillators is their use in providing divergence signals. Divergences can provide important clues as to the possible direction of near-future momentum. This

148

concept of divergences is touched on in this chapter's Tips and Techniques section.

Divergences

Price-oscillator divergences are instances when there is a technical imbalance between price movement and an oscillator's movement. Divergences should not be considered complete, self-contained trading strategies. Rather, they should be regarded as signals that warn of some potential impending directional bias. As such, divergences are not stand-alone indicators—they should confirm or be confirmed by other technical indications.

The oscillator that is used to identify divergences can be any of a number of different chart studies that can be found on any charting platform. These include stochastics, relative strength index (RSI), moving average convergence/divergence (MACD), MACD histogram, rate of change (ROC), momentum, commodity channel index (CCI), Williams %R, or any other oscillator that travels between defined horizontal bounds.

Once an oscillator is chosen, the process of searching for divergences is straightforward. There are two types of divergence that every technical trader should be aware of: regular divergence and hidden divergence.

Regular divergence is the most popular type, and it is what most traders mean when they refer to the general concept of divergence. Regular divergence serves as an early potential signal that a loss of momentum and a potential price reversal may be in the making.

The signal is manifested in an uptrend when price makes a higher high while the oscillator makes a lower high. This is called bearish regular divergence, and warns of a potential reversal and

TIPS AND TECHNIQUES (CONTINUED)

possible subsequent move to the downside. The opposite is called bullish regular divergence and occurs during downtrends. In a bullish divergence, price makes a lower low while the oscillator makes a higher low. In both cases, bearish and bullish, the oscillator diverges from price, giving an indication that price momentum in the currently prevailing direction may be waning.

If either type of regular divergence is identified on a chart, traders should immediately seek confirmation of a potential reversal before taking any trading action. This confirmation can take many forms and usually involves a combination of other technical indications, such as a trend line or moving average break, a reversal candle pattern, or some other chart reversal pattern.

In contrast to regular divergence, the second type of divergence, called hidden divergence, can be considered the polar opposite. This signal is also a technical imbalance between price movement and oscillator movement. But instead of signaling a potential reversal, hidden divergence is used primarily to signal a potential continuation in the prevailing trend. As with regular divergence, there are also two basic manifestations of hidden divergence.

Bearish hidden divergence usually occurs during a downtrend and is characterized by price making a lower high while the oscillator makes a higher high. In this case, price and the oscillator are diverging in their signals, but the overriding signal that should be taken from an occurrence of bearish hidden divergence is a potential continuation of the lower highs in price, which is the equivalent of a potential continuation in the prevailing downtrend. Bullish hidden divergence usually occurs during an uptrend and is characterized by price making a higher low while the oscillator makes a lower low. In this case, price and the oscillator are diverging in their signals, but the overriding signal that should be taken from an occurrence of bullish hidden divergence is a potential continuation of the higher lows in price, which is the equivalent of a potential continuation in the prevailing uptrend.

As with regular divergence, confirmation should also be sought for instances of hidden divergence before any trades are actually placed. This confirmation can also take many forms and usually involves a combination of other technical indications that point to a potential continuation of the prevailing trend.

Divergences are common and useful signals that are best utilized as warnings, or confirmations, of potential reversals (regular divergence) or potential trend continuations (hidden divergence).

The relative strength index, as shown in Exhibit 10.8, is yet another popular indicator introduced by J. Welles Wilder in his 1978 book, *New Concepts in Technical Trading Systems*. This oscillator is among the most widely used by technical traders in all financial markets. Some innovative traders have developed this tool far beyond its original purposes, to serve as a primary trading tool almost as important as price action itself. Others use RSI as a key confirmation tool on the bottom of their charts.

During horizontal ranging markets, RSI is a classic oscillator that excels at providing a measure of price momentum as well as providing overbought and oversold indications. In this way, it utilizes the same concept of reversion to the mean that is behind the linear regression indicator. Mathematically, the RSI is simply a comparison of the magnitude of recent gains to recent losses, with a formula that looks like this:

$$100/(1 + RS)$$

where $RS =$ average of x periods closes up divided by the average of
x periods closes down

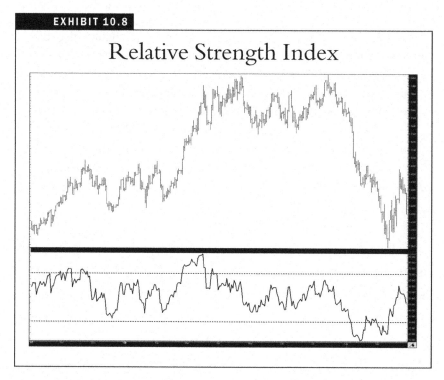

EXHIBIT 10.8

Relative Strength Index

Source: FX Solutions—FX AccuCharts

The x number of periods is the primary RSI setting, which is usually set at a default of 14 periods but can be changed readily. Also by default, the overbought and oversold boundaries are usually set at 70 and 30, respectively. A cross above the 70 level is considered an indication of price being potentially overbought, while a cross below the 30 level is considered an indication of price being potentially oversold.

Some technical traders use RSI as a trade signaling and confirmation tool in this manner. Potential long trades in a ranging market would be confirmed on a cross of the RSI from the oversold region above the 30 level. Potential short trades in a ranging market would

EXHIBIT 10.9

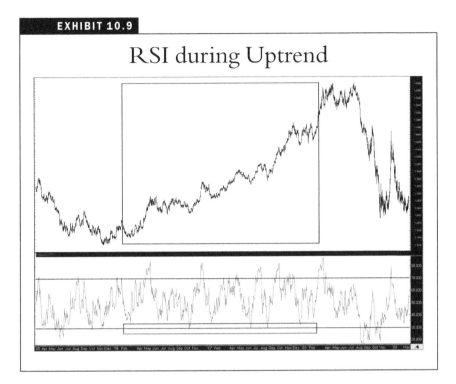

RSI during Uptrend

Source: FX Solutions—FX AccuCharts

be confirmed on a cross of the RSI from the overbought region below the 70 level.

During trending markets, RSI can also serve as a useful oscillator. Innovative technical analysts have made certain observations regarding RSI during trends. Perhaps the most important of these observations is that RSI often fails to reach the oversold area during uptrends (see Exhibit 10.9) and, conversely, fails to reach the overbought area during downtrends (see Exhibit 10.10). This is a readily observable phenomenon that can be measured with a horizontal line well above 30 or well below 70. The RSI oscillator's tendency to do

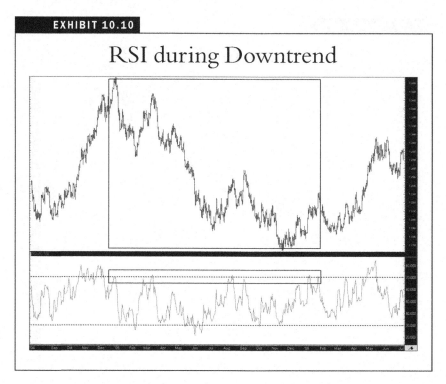

EXHIBIT 10.10

RSI during Downtrend

Source: FX Solutions—FX AccuCharts

this can help both in identifying trends in a market as well as in pinpointing entries into a trending market.

The stochastics oscillator was introduced in the 1950s by George Lane, a trader and pioneering technical analyst, and is therefore often referred to as Lane's stochastics. Generally two different varieties of stochastics can be found on most charting software: fast and slow. Slow stochastics, as shown in Exhibit 10.11, is simply a smoothed version of fast stochastics. Whichever variety is chosen, the purpose is similar to other oscillators: Identify overbought/oversold and provide divergence signals.

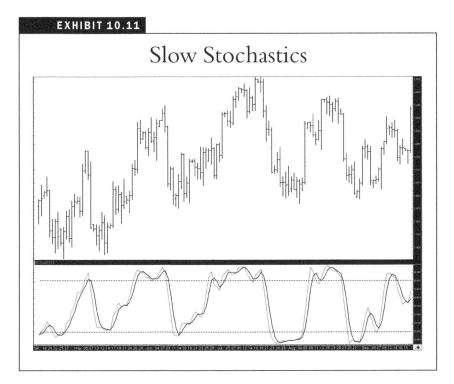

EXHIBIT 10.11

Slow Stochastics

Source: FX Solutions—FX AccuCharts

The mathematical formula for stochastics compares the currency pair's closing price to its price range over a set period of time. The primary concept behind this oscillator is that prices tend to close near recent highs during bull markets and near recent lows during bear markets. There are two lines that are calculated for stochastics: %K (fast) and %D (slow). These lines travel between the extremes of 0 and 100, where the default oversold and overbought levels are generally set at 20 and 80, respectively. The calculation of %K is:

$$100 \times [(C - Ln)/(Hn - Ln)]$$

where   C = most recent closing price

Ln = low of the last n days

Hn = high of the last n days

%D is simply a moving average of %K, which is usually set at a three-period moving average.

Because stochastics has two lines as opposed to RSI's one line, stochastics can give off an additional signal that results when the %K line crosses the %D line, much in the same way that trading signals are derived from moving average crossovers.

Rate of change, as shown in Exhibit 10.12, is a very simple and classic oscillator that provides a basic momentum measure. The

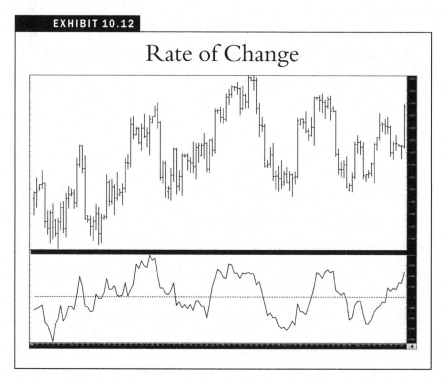

EXHIBIT 10.12

Rate of Change

Source: FX Solutions—FX AccuCharts

mathematical calculation for this oscillator measures the percent change from the price a given number of periods ago to the current price. The equation for ROC is:

$$100 \times [(Cc - Cn)/(Cn)]$$

where   Cc = close of the current price bar
Cn = close of the bar n periods ago

Like many other oscillators, the default setting for this given number of periods is often 14 but can be changed readily. ROC oscillates above and below a zero line and so has both positive and negative values.

Besides showing divergence and overbought/oversold conditions, ROC can also provide possible trading signals when the oscillator goes above and below the zero line.

The commodity channel index oscillator, as shown in Exhibit 10.13, is an important but perhaps misnamed oscillator that was first introduced by Donald Lambert in 1980. Just as comfortable in the major markets of stocks, bonds, and currencies as it is in the futures/commodities arena, CCI has proven itself to be a popular oscillator with many traders in all financial markets. Originally intended to identify cycles in the commodities markets, CCI has grown to become a highly valued tool for identifying and confirming potential price turns.

The mathematical purpose of CCI is to derive the relationship among price, a moving average of price, and deviations from that average. The equation is:

$$(Price - MA)/(0.015 \times D)$$

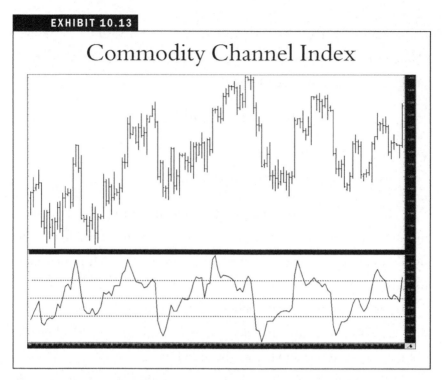

EXHIBIT 10.13

Commodity Channel Index

Source: FX Solutions—FX AccuCharts

where Price = typical price (average of high, low, and closing prices)

MA = simple moving average

D = mean absolute deviation

Typically, CCI oscillates above and below a zero line, and over-bought/oversold levels are usually set at +100 and −100, respectively.

CCI adherents, much like those who follow every move made by the RSI, have invented many different methods of analyzing this oscillator above and beyond its conventional use of identifying divergences and overbought/oversold conditions. As with the RSI oscillator, a small but prominent community of traders concentrates on the patterns and movements of the CCI alone, often even to the exclusion of viewing price itself. But even when this oscillator is employed merely as a secondary confirming indicator, its worth has been well established in the eyes of many who have experimented with it.

Most technical traders have gravitated toward their favorite oscillator(s) through extensive experimentation and observation. Like other types of indicators, oscillators can be extremely useful complements to all of the other technical tools available to traders and investors through their charting software.

The precisely derived behavior of mathematical indicators and oscillators stands in stark contrast to the decidedly less objective methods surrounding such charting tools as Fibonacci and Elliott Wave. This is not at all to say that one tool is any better than another. Different traders and investors have found different value in the various available analysis tools, whether these tools are considered to be more subjective or more objective. Some traders gravitate toward mathematically complex indicators, while others find success with more subjective trend line analyses. Yet other traders combine the strengths of a variety of analysis tools.

Because of the importance of Fibonacci and Elliott Wave studies, an entire chapter is devoted to them. They are the subject of Chapter 11.

Summary

This chapter introduced some of the key indicators and oscillators used in technical analysis. Indicators are mathematically derived representations of price that can give clues as to price volatility, momentum, and trend. Like moving averages, indicators and oscillators have the weakness that they are generally lagging, which means they only follow price action and cannot actually forecast price action. Oscillators are a special subset of indicators that give readings of momentum and price-oscillator divergence.

Key indicators used in all major financial markets include MACD, Bollinger Bands, ADX, ATR, parabolic SAR, and linear regression, among many others. Key oscillators include RSI, stochastics, ROC, CCI, momentum, and Williams %R, among several others.

CHAPTER 11

Fibonacci and Elliott Wave

After reading this chapter, you will be able to:

- Discern the unique bases, characteristics, and interpretations of both Fibonacci theory and Elliott Wave theory in technical analysis.

- Begin applying the theories of Fibonacci and Elliott Wave to analyze and trade the financial markets.

- Know the most fundamental rules and tools used to implement these unique theories.

Fibonacci Theory and Methods

Fibonacci and Elliott Wave are two well-developed and closely interrelated perspectives for analyzing market price action. While they can certainly be used in isolation, their utility is usually considered to be magnified when used in conjunction with each other. In this chapter, the tenets and characteristics of both Fibonacci theory and Elliott Wave theory are discussed separately.

The concepts and theories of Fibonacci originated from a thirteenth-century Italian mathematician by the name of Leonardo of Pisa, otherwise known as Leonardo Fibonacci. His work that eventually led to such mainstream technical analysis standards as Fibonacci retracements stemmed from a sequence of numbers that led to the discovery of the Golden Ratio, approximately 1.618. This ratio, as Fibonacci advocates claim, can be found in all of nature, science, music, and, most importantly, even financial markets.

The Fibonacci sequence of numbers, which were introduced to the Western world in Fibonacci's 1202 book *Liber Abaci*, are, in part: 0, 1, 1, 2, 3, 5, 8, 13, 21, 34, 55, 89, 144, 233, 377, 610, 987, 1597. . . . An interesting characteristic of this sequence is that the sum of each two consecutive numbers results in the next number in the series: 0+1=1, 1+1=2, 1+2=3, 2+3=5, 3+5=8, and so on. Another interesting characteristic is that as the Fibonacci sequence progresses to greater values, the ratio of one number to the one before it progressively approaches the Golden Ratio of 1.618.

Because this ratio purportedly exists in many areas of the natural and man-made worlds, it was only a matter of time before this theory would be applied to the financial markets. This application has now become a standard technical tool on virtually all financial charting platforms.

The primary, and most basic, purpose of Fibonacci analysis is to determine potential areas of trend retracement. As discussed in Chapter 5, on uptrends and downtrends, all financial markets experience certain periods in which price is moving generally in one direction, whether it is to the upside or to the downside. These net directional price movements are called trends. Although trends may move in one general direction, there are always periods of correction, or retracement, where price moves in a countertrend fashion. In an established uptrend, for example, there are always plenty of down-moves that retrace a portion of the prior up-move. It is simply the nature of all financial markets that price does not move in only one direction for any extended length of time.

As this is the case, there will always be dips during uptrends and rallies during downtrends. These areas of price action are among the most advantageous locations to enter trades in the direction of the prevailing trend. In an uptrend, for example, the goal is generally to buy low and sell high. Buying on a minor price dip affords the potentially beneficial opportunity to enter into an uptrend trade at a relatively low price. Conversely, in a downtrend, the goal is generally to sell (short) high and then buy back (cover) low. Selling on a minor price rally affords the potentially beneficial opportunity to enter into a downtrend trade at a relatively high price. It follows that it would be advantageous for traders to prepare themselves ahead of time by having a good idea of where price retracements may likely stop and turn back in the direction of the trend. These traders would then have the opportunity to place high-probability trades in the direction of the trend after a countertrend retracement.

This is the primary concept behind Fibonacci retracement analysis. The main Fibonacci retracement percentages are based on the inverse of the 1.618 Golden Ratio, namely 0.618, or 61.8 percent. Besides this important percentage, there is the key 38.2 percent, which adds up with 61.8 percent to equal 100 percent. The third most important Fibonacci retracement percentage is 50 percent. Other commonly used percentages include 23.6 percent and 76.4 percent, which, when added up, also equal 100 percent. To summarize, the most popular Fibonacci retracement levels that are watched by the vast majority of traders who use Fibonacci are 38.2 percent, 61.8 percent, and 50 percent. There are also those who watch the 23.6 percent and 76.4 percent levels.

Many people who are unfamiliar with the applications of Fibonacci retracements wonder why price action often reacts significantly to these retracement percentages and why so many traders believe in what appear, on the surface, simply to be magic numbers. One component of what makes Fibonacci tools work surprisingly well under diverse market conditions is the simple fact that many traders, both large and small, utilize Fibonacci in their trading. As a result, the levels derived from these popular retracement percentages have become somewhat of a self-fulfilling prophecy. Therefore, significant price action, such as price turns, often occurs around these levels due partly to the fact that many traders are watching and reacting to these price levels. This phenomenon contributes, at least partially, to their frequent effectiveness and accuracy in describing market movements.

As shown in Exhibit 11.1, Fibonacci retracement percentages are often used to locate potential bounces in price action where traders may wish to enter into a trend on a countertrend retracement. For example, in a major uptrend situation where price has been making a bearish correction, many traders would be looking first for a potential bounce around the 38.2 percent level of the original uptrend move. If evidence of a potential bounce around this level is sufficient, these traders may enter into long trades, further pushing price up in a

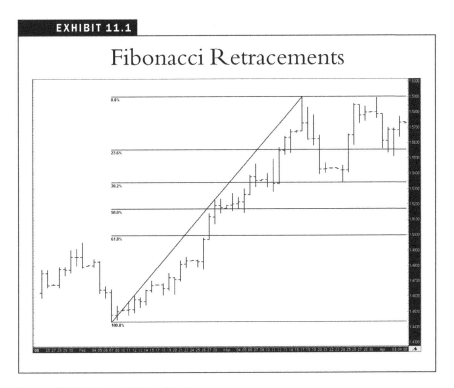

EXHIBIT 11.1

Fibonacci Retracements

Source: FX Solutions—FX AccuCharts

bounce up off the 38.2 percent level. Besides being traded in this fashion, Fibonacci levels may also be considered areas of potential breakouts. In the same trend retracement scenario just described, if instead of bouncing up off the 38.2 level, price instead broke down cleanly below that level, it would represent a potential breakout trading opportunity in the direction of the countertrend retracement. Fibonacci retracement levels can also be used as profit targets for existing open trades.

Besides the Fibonacci internal percentages of 23.6 percent, 38.2 percent, 50 percent, 61.8 percent, and 76.4 percent, there are also Fibonacci extensions that extend beyond 100 percent, as shown

EXHIBIT 11.2

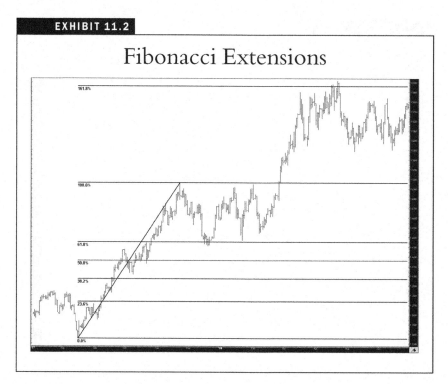

Fibonacci Extensions

Source: FX Solutions—FX AccuCharts

in Exhibit 11.2. These extensions are used primarily for determining and forecasting price targets. The most important Fibonacci extension percentages are 161.8 percent, which represents the Golden Ratio, and 261.8 percent. Fibonacci extensions are often used in triangle pattern situations, where the trader is looking for a potential price target after the triangle is broken. Both Fibonacci retracements and Fibonacci extensions are highly configurable on most charting platforms.

Besides retracements and extensions, several other Fibonacci tools are routinely included on chart software for any financial market. One of these is the Fibonacci fan, as shown in Exhibit 11.3. This

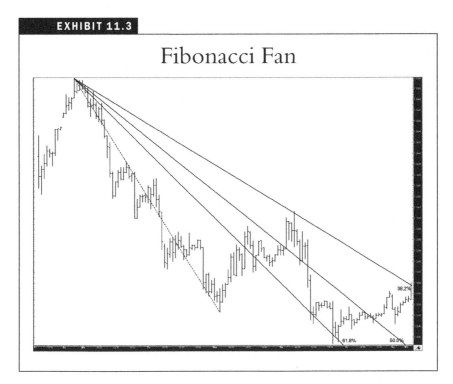

EXHIBIT 11.3

Fibonacci Fan

Source: FX Solutions—FX AccuCharts

relatively common Fibonacci tool draws a "fan" of three diagonal lines that represent possible dynamic support and resistance levels. These levels are based on the three key Fibonacci ratios of 38.2 percent, 50 percent, and 61.8 percent. Much like Fibonacci retracements, the levels are derived by drawing a straight line from a major swing low to a major swing high, or vice versa. The charting software then automatically derives these Fibonacci levels.

Instead of fanned straight lines, the Fibonacci arc, as shown in Exhibit 11.4, draws three curved arc lines that also determine regions of potential support and/or resistance. Much like the Fibonacci fan, the Fibonacci arc has lines that are based on the key Fibonacci ratios

EXHIBIT 11.4

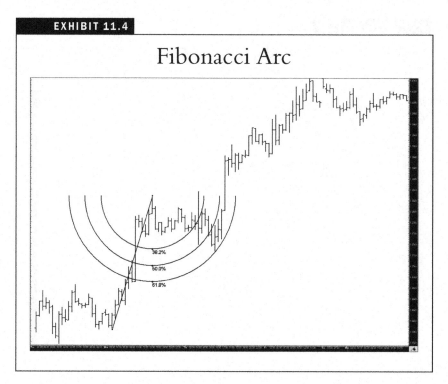

Fibonacci Arc

Source: FX Solutions—FX AccuCharts

of 38.2 percent, 50 percent, and 61.8 percent. Additionally, like the Fibonacci fan lines, the Fibonacci arc lines are derived by drawing a straight line from a major swing low to a major swing high, or vice versa. (As a side note, Robert Prechter, Jr., noted Elliott Wave authority, considers Fibonacci arcs as well as Gann angles to be invalid because their outcomes are based on arbitrary scaling choices.)

Although also based on Fibonacci theory, Fibonacci time zones, as shown in Exhibit 11.5, are significantly different from retracements, fans, and arcs. Instead of being based directly on ratios, Fibonacci time zones are based on the Fibonacci number sequence (1, 2, 3, 5, 8, 13, 21, 34, 55, 89, 144, 233, etc.) described earlier in

EXHIBIT 11.5

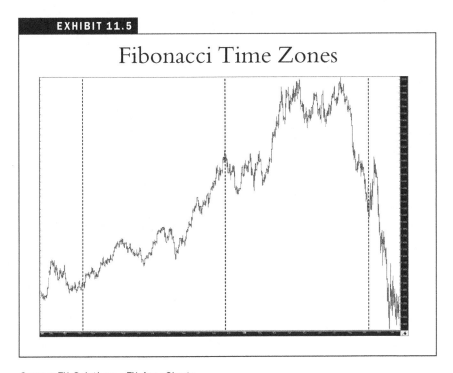

Fibonacci Time Zones

Source: FX Solutions—FX AccuCharts

this chapter. Generally, a trader would choose a starting point on the chart after some major price move. The Fibonacci time zones tool would then automatically plot vertical lines on the chart after the starting point, based on time periods that correspond with the Fibonacci number sequence. The expectation is that the vertical lines help pinpoint times in the future when there could potentially be a substantial technical event or price movement.

There are certainly other charting tools based on Fibonacci theory, but the most common and popular ones, as well as the ones most likely to be found on most charting platforms, are those that have just been described. By far, the Fibonacci tool followed by the greatest number of traders would have to be the Fibonacci retracements. Fibonacci retracements also play a substantial role in the basis and application of Elliott Wave theory, which is covered next.

Elliott Wave Theory

Named after and originated by famed stock market analyst Ralph Nelson Elliott, the body of knowledge known as Elliott Wave theory seeks to forecast financial market movement by defining price action according to certain identifiable wave patterns. Elliott introduced his theories in the late 1930s after having studied decades' worth of stock market price data. Much later, Elliott's work was further refined by Robert Prechter, Jr., a trader and analyst who became well known for his market timing and trading acumen using Elliott Wave principles.

The primary principle behind Elliott Wave is that market behavior is governed by cause-and-effect forces that produce certain identifiable, and ultimately predictable, patterns. These patterns manifest themselves in the form of waves, which are simply directional movements of price in a financial market.

A price action cycle is composed of two sets of waves, as illustrated in Exhibit 11.6. The first set is called motive and includes five waves that make up an overall trend movement. The second set is called corrective and includes three waves that make up an overall countertrend, or corrective, movement.

Within the five waves that make up the overall motive trend movement, three of them (waves 1, 3, and 5) are actually in the direction of the trend. They are also called motive waves because they

EXHIBIT 11.6

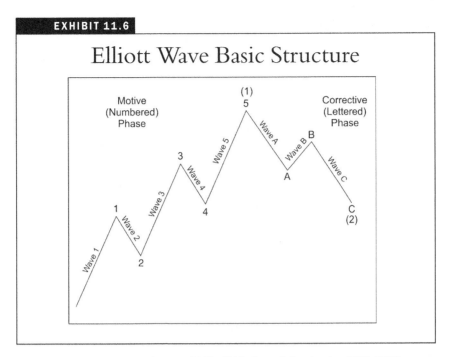

Elliott Wave Basic Structure

move in the direction of the trend. Two of the waves (waves 2 and 4) within the overall motive trend movement are against the trend and are therefore called corrective. Waves 2 and 4 retrace a portion of the gains made during the immediately preceding trend movement.

Within the three waves that make up the overall corrective movement, two of them (waves A and C) are in the direction of the new countertrend movement, and are called motive because they move in the same direction as the new corrective trend. The second wave (wave B) within this overall corrective movement, which only retraces a portion of wave A, is against the new trend and is therefore called corrective. Exhibit 11.7 illustrates these principles in detail.

EXHIBIT 11.7

Elliott Wave Comprehensive Structure

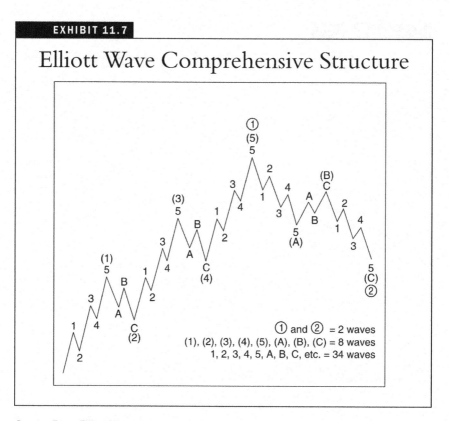

① and ② = 2 waves
(1), (2), (3), (4), (5), (A), (B), (C) = 8 waves
1, 2, 3, 4, 5, A, B, C, etc. = 34 waves

Source: From *Elliott Wave Principle* (1978–2009, Frost & Prechter) © 1978–2009.
Used with permission.

The main principle behind this wave structure is that a price movement cycle is made up of eight waves. Price action in the direction of the larger trend is comprised of five waves (three with the trend and two against the trend), while corrective price movement against the larger trend is comprised of three waves (two with the countertrend and one against the countertrend).

Very importantly, within each individual wave is a smaller subwave structure that also adheres to the 5/3 wave pattern, depending on whether the wave is with the larger trend or against it. So the basic

5/3 pattern remains intact on every magnitude, from the longest term to the shortest term, and each wave pattern exists within the context of a larger wave pattern while also encompassing many smaller wave patterns. Exhibit 11.7 illustrates this structure within a structure within a structure.

For the five-wave motive trend pattern, there are three simple guidelines that should not be violated when applying Elliott Wave theory to financial price charts:

1. Wave 2 never moves beyond the beginning of Wave 1.

2. Wave 3 is never the shortest wave.

3. Wave 4 never enters the price span of Wave 1.

Elliott Wave theory also includes several key elements that are mainstays of the broader field of general technical analysis. These elements include such important chart patterns as triangles, wedges, and parallel trend channels. With regard to the concept of channels, Elliott Wave theory asserts that trending price action often conforms remarkably well to the shape of a parallel trend channel and that these channels can be used to locate high-probability price targets for the various waves. In a five-wave pattern, for example, after the first, second, and third waves have completed, a line can be drawn from the end of wave 1 to the end of wave 3. A second line parallel to this first line can then be drawn that encompasses the endpoint of wave 2. This channeling process provides an initial estimated target for wave 4. Of course, in order to retain their targeting properties, trend channels must often be adjusted and redrawn according to how the waves actually unfold. Channeling can serve exceptionally well as a method for describing and targeting price action within trends.

Another key concept of Elliott Wave theory is called alternation. This term refers to the observed phenomenon that waves that are structurally similar, such as corrective waves 2 and 4 within a five-wave pattern, tend to differ and alternate in the nature of their expression. To use the example of waves 2 and 4, if wave 2 represents a steep correction of the prior wave, wave 4 (which is a similar corrective wave to wave 2) should not be expected to be yet another steep corrective wave. Rather, according to the Elliott Wave principle of alternation, wave 4 should alternate in its expression and therefore manifest itself as a flatter, or more horizontal, corrective wave. Alternation is one of the primary guidelines of Elliott Wave theory as it is one of the most consistent principles of market price action.

Even these bare essentials of Elliott Wave theory may be complex and perhaps overwhelming to new traders and investors. Therefore, although there are many more nuances and intricacies involved with true Elliott Wave analysis, many who try their hand at this type of financial analysis never get much beyond the 5/3 wave counting. If a new trader is able to master this art of wave counting and actually apply it to charts under all market conditions, that trader will have made a very substantial head start in learning how financial markets are structured and, perhaps more important, in making informed decisions on possible market directions.

In the hands of skilled practitioners, both Fibonacci applications and Elliott Wave theory can be extremely powerful tools for speculating in the financial markets. These and other technical studies form the basis for many effective technical trading strategies, whether they are executed manually by a trader or automatically by a computer trading platform. Select trading strategies are the subject of

Chapter 14. Before that, however, the process and strategy involved in analyzing point-and-figure charts are covered in Chapter 12.

Summary

This chapter provided basic introductions to the key concepts of Fibonacci theory and Elliott Wave theory. Both of these closely related sets of principles are used extensively by many technical analysts, traders, and investors.

Fibonacci numbers and ratios are based on the Golden Ratio and the work of a thirteenth-century mathematician known as Leonardo Fibonacci. Fibonacci ratios occur in nature, science, and music, and were thus adapted to the financial markets. The most common use of Fibonacci ratios is to identify potential trend retracements. They are also commonly used for identifying price targets in the form of Fibonacci extensions. Besides the very prevalent Fibonacci retracement drawing tool, which is offered by virtually all major charting software, other drawing tools that utilize Fibonacci principles include the Fibonacci fan, the Fibonacci arc, and Fibonacci time zones.

Elliott Wave theory is a more complex set of principles that was introduced in the 1930s by Ralph Nelson Elliott. This theory puts forth a concrete structural view of financial markets. The structure includes well-defined price waves as well as guidelines to govern how those waves should act and react with each other. The Elliott Wave view of financial markets, much like Fibonacci methodology, has been widely adopted by professional technical traders.

CHAPTER 12

Point-and-Figure Charting

After reading this chapter, you will be able to:

- Understand what sets point-and-figure charts apart from other, more conventional charting methods.
- Appreciate the unique structure and characteristics of point-and-figure charts that allow them to facilitate pure price action trading.
- Apply point and figure patterns to practical trading in any financial market.

Introduction to Point and Figure

Point-and-figure (p&f) charts are an older form of charting that originated in the nineteenth century as a method for plotting market prices. As noted in Chapter 4, p&f charts are one of the major forms of charting, aside from bar charts, candlestick charts, and line charts.

Also as noted, p&f charts differ drastically from bar charts, candlestick charts, and line charts in both their appearance as well as their functionality.

Point-and-figure charts have always had their loyal adherents. Although this charting method has been eclipsed in the present-day by other charting forms, at least in terms of popularity, p&f charts offer a truly unique and efficient representation of market prices that is the method of choice for many traders and investors around the world involved in all financial markets.

Trading with p&f charts is akin to trading purely off of price action. This is due to the fact that only the most important data point for any given financial instrument—price—is recorded on these charts. Excluded are all of the other data points that are normally included on bar and candlestick charts, namely time, volume, and period opens, highs, lows, and closes. Without all of these other data points to clutter up the analytical landscape, all that remains is pure price action. This, in turn, clarifies the two essential dynamics of trend and support/resistance in a significant manner.

One of the primary factors that differentiate point-and-figure charts from other types of charts is appearance. Unlike those other types of charts, p&f charts consist of a grid of boxes, as shown in Exhibit 12.1. The y-axis, as in other types of charts, represents price. Unlike other charts, however, the x-axis does not represent time but instead represents simply a progression of columns moving from left to right.

Within each of these columns is a vertical line of either Xs or Os. The rightmost column represents the current price action, whether it is a column of Xs or Os. A vertical column of Xs simply means that

EXHIBIT 12.1

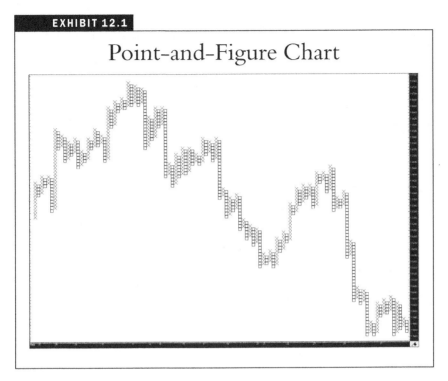

Point-and-Figure Chart

Source: FX Solutions—FX AccuCharts

price has had a net increase. Conversely, a column of Os simply means that price has had a net decrease. So, for example, if price trends up by a certain minimum price amount, a column of Xs will begin forming. Then, if price reverses and begins to trend down by a certain minimum price amount, the column of Xs will end, and a new column of Os will begin on the immediate right-hand side of the column of Xs. These X and O columns continue moving right and alternating with each other as the swings and turns of price action progresses. Unlike in other types of charts, p&f charts will not progress to the right unless there are significant price turns or reversals that necessitate the creation of new X and O columns.

There are two primary variables when setting up a typical point-and-figure chart. These variables allow p&f charts the advantage of filtering out the noise fluctuations in price that plague other types of charts.

The first variable is box size. This is the minimum increment that price needs to move before another X is added on top of an X column, or another O is added to the bottom of an O column. Determination of the box size depends entirely on the particular financial instrument traded and the amount of noise reduction desired. If, for example, a column of Xs has formed, that column will not grow an additional X on the top if price has not moved by the minimum box size price increment. If the minimum box size price increment is reached, one X will be added onto the top of the column.

The other primary variable for point-and-figure charts is reversal amount. This is another noise reduction feature to decrease the amount of price fluctuations on the charts, thereby providing a clearer trend and reversal picture. The most popular setting for this variable is the three-point reversal. A three-point reversal simply means that a new column of Os (after an X column) or a new column of Xs (after an O column) will not be started unless the price reverses from the peak of the current column by a minimum threshold of three boxes. Any price move of less than this three-box minimum is considered noise and is ignored by the p&f chart. This feature greatly decreases incidences of minor price oscillations giving false reversal readings. When price fails to reverse by the three-box minimum threshold, a column of Xs remains as is, without adding a new O column. Likewise, a column of Os remains as is, without adding a new X column.

With these two basic variables of box size and reversal amount, p&f charts are able to point out and clarify trending price action exceptionally well. These charts also excel at delineating support and resistance zones as well as highlighting high-probability breakout trading opportunities.

Point-and-Figure Patterns

An abundance of chart patterns unique to point-and-figure charts enable traders and investors to take advantage of potential breakout trading opportunities. In addition, while some chart patterns, like the ubiquitous double top, are considered reversal patterns by bar and candlestick practitioners, they are considered breakout patterns by p&f adherents. This holds true for double tops and bottoms as well as triple tops and bottoms. Besides chart patterns, p&f trading strategies also involve trend line and trend channel breaks. Along with the chart patterns, these are illustrated and described in this chapter.

Perhaps the simplest of all p&f chart patterns is the double-top/double-bottom pattern, as illustrated in Exhibits 12.2 and 12.3. As mentioned, this popular pattern generally means the opposite on p&f charts as it does on the standard bar or candlestick chart. Like all common p&f patterns, a double top or double bottom is a breakout signal and should be treated as a breakout trading opportunity.

As an example of a double-top pattern, suppose an X column is in place and then reverses by the minimum reversal threshold of three boxes, thereby forming a new O column and establishing a top on the X column. Then suppose that after this occurs, price reverses again to create yet another X column. When this new X column

EXHIBIT 12.2

Double Top Breakout

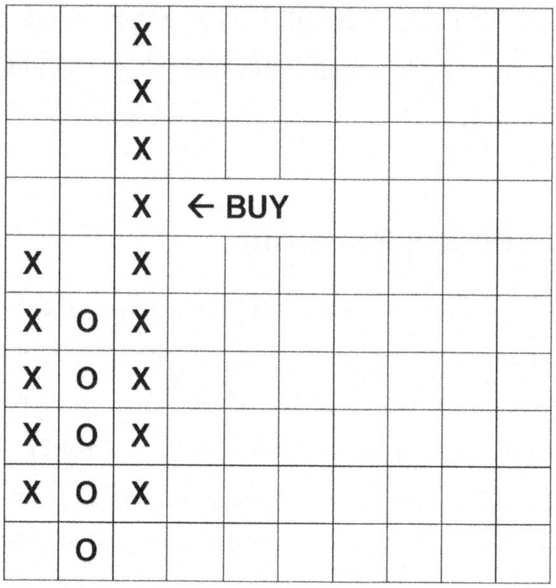

		X							
		X							
		X							
		X	← BUY						
X		X							
X	O	X							
X	O	X							
X	O	X							
X	O	X							
	O								

reaches the same box price level as the previous X column, a double top is established. Then, instead of a reversal, the key event to watch for would be a breakout above the previous X column, which would be evident if a new X formed above the previous X column's high. On this type of price action, the signal given would be a buy, or long, on the breakout. The same price action, but in reverse, would describe a double-bottom breakdown trading opportunity.

Another simple p&f chart pattern, as shown in Exhibits 12.4 and 12.5, is the triple-top/triple-bottom pattern. Like the double-top/double-bottom pattern, this pattern generally means the opposite on p&f charts as it does on the standard bar or candlestick chart. On p&f

EXHIBIT 12.3

Double Bottom Breakdown

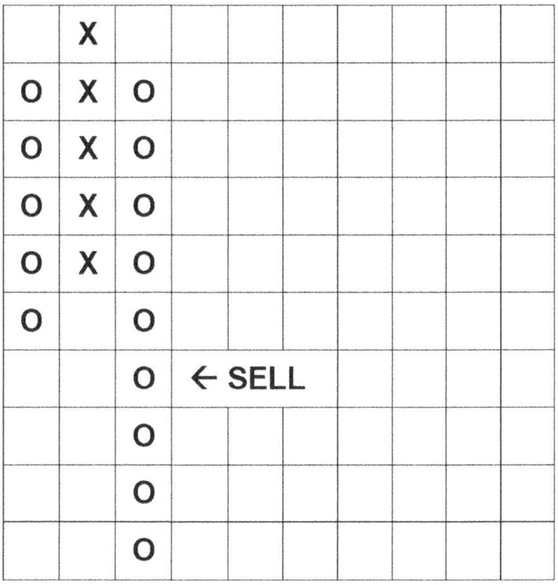

	X								
O	X	O							
O	X	O							
O	X	O							
O	X	O							
O		O							
		O	← SELL						
		O							
		O							
		O							

charts, a triple top or triple bottom is a signal to watch for a breakout trading opportunity.

For example, suppose there is an X column, then an O column, and then another X column that reaches the same box price level as the first X column. Then suppose another O column appears and then finally another X column. On this fifth column, or third X column, if it reaches up to the box price level of both the first and second X column, that is called a triple top. Then, instead of a price reversal, the key event to be watching for, as with double tops, would be a breakout above the two previous X highs. This would give a signal to buy, or go long, on the breakout. The same price action,

EXHIBIT 12.4

Triple Top Breakout

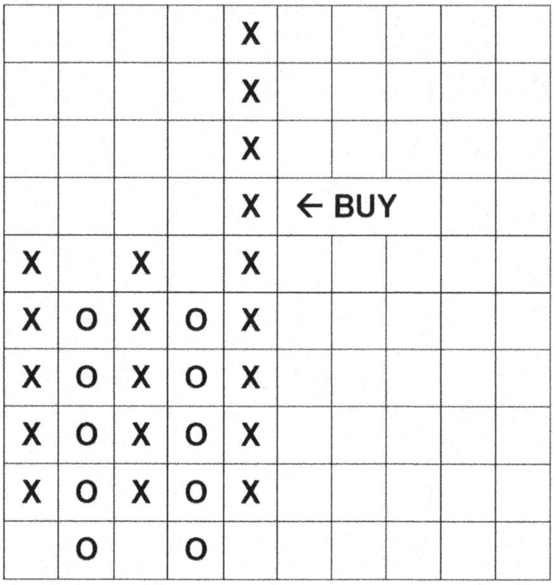

			X						
			X						
			X						
			X	← BUY					
X		X	X						
X	O	X	O	X					
X	O	X	O	X					
X	O	X	O	X					
X	O	X	O	X					
	O		O						

but in reverse, would describe a triple-bottom breakdown trading opportunity.

As on bar and candlestick charts, dynamic trend line breakouts and breakdowns are relatively common occurrences on p&f charts. For the most part, p&f trend line breaks, as shown in Exhibits 12.6 and 12.7, work on the same principles as trend line breaks on other types of charts. The only exception is that trend lines on p&f charts are usually drawn only at 45-degree angles. This prerequisite creates a stricter environment for the drawing of trend lines but also fosters more precision when depicting trend line breaks.

EXHIBIT 12.5

Triple Bottom Breakdown

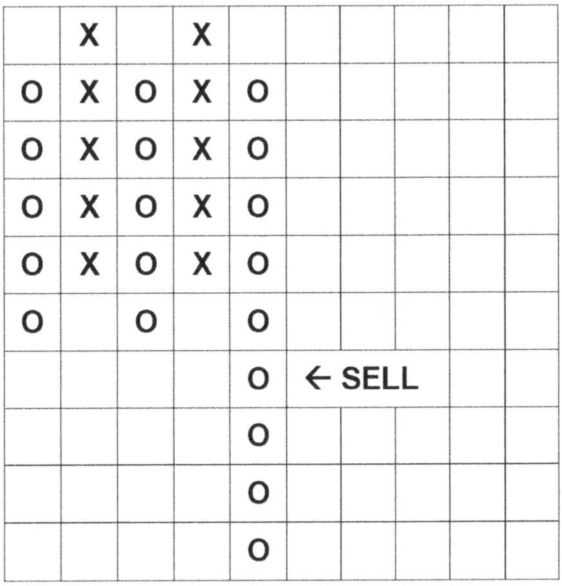

	X		X						
O	X	O	X	O					
O	X	O	X	O					
O	X	O	X	O					
O	X	O	X	O					
O		O		O					
				O	← SELL				
				O					
				O					
				O					

As on other types of charts, an uptrend line generally runs underneath rising price action, providing price with a dynamically ascending floor of support. A breakdown below such an uptrend line is a signal of a potential trend reversal. Likewise, a downtrend line generally runs above falling price action, providing price with a dynamically descending ceiling of resistance. A breakout above such a downtrend line is a signal of a potential trend reversal. When a breakdown below a 45-degree uptrend support line occurs, or a breakout above a 45-degree downtrend resistance line occurs, these are potential signs that price carries the countertrend strength and

EXHIBIT 12.6

Breakout above Bearish Resistance Downtrend Line

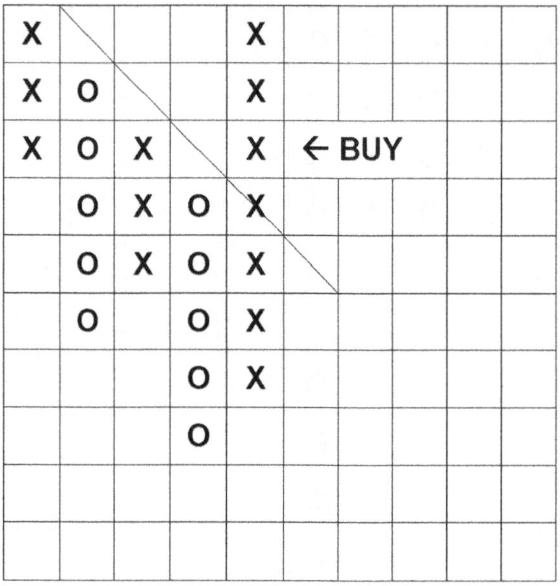

X				X					
X	O			X					
X	O	X		X	← BUY				
	O	X	O	X					
	O	X	O	X					
	O		O	X					
			O	X					
			O						

momentum to reverse the previously prevailing trend, thereby rewarding those who take part in the breakout opportunity.

Like trend lines on p&f charts, symmetrical triangles are characterized by 45-degree angles, as shown in Exhibits 12.8 and 12.9. Ascending and descending triangles can also occur but are less common. Symmetrical triangles are also not exceptionally common on p&f charts, but when they are found, they can be very useful in their breakout potential.

In the same fashion as with ascending and descending 45-degree trend lines, breaks of triangles are of two primary types. A bullish

EXHIBIT 12.7

Breakdown below Bullish Support Uptrend Line

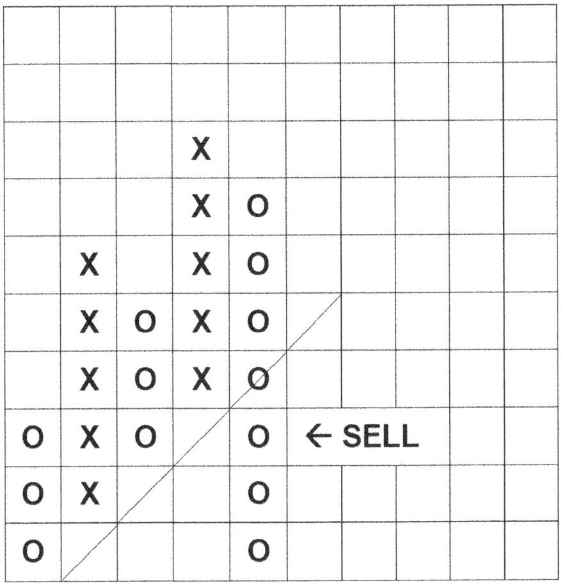

		X						
		X	O					
	X	X	O					
	X	O	X	O				
	X	O	X	O				
O	X	O		O	← SELL			
O	X			O				
O				O				

breakout above a symmetrical triangle is essentially the same as a bullish breakout above a 45-degree descending resistance trend line. Similarly, a bearish breakdown below a symmetrical triangle is essentially the same as a bearish breakdown below a 45-degree ascending support trend line. Either way, the break of an angled trend line, or a triangle border, is considered a significant trade entry signal.

Other point-and-figure chart patterns are similar in nature to those described in this chapter. The ultimate goal for traders and investors who watch all of these patterns is to exploit the violation of support/resistance, whether that support/resistance is in static form,

EXHIBIT 12.8

Bullish Breakout above Symmetrical Triangle

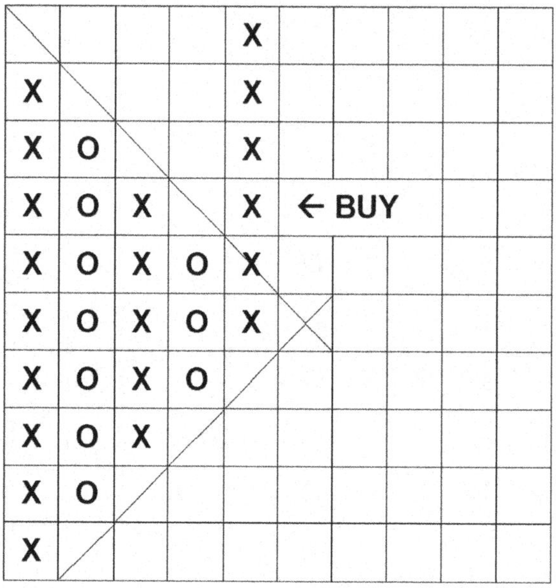

				X					
X				X					
X	O			X					
X	O	X		X	← BUY				
X	O	X	O	X					
X	O	X	O	X					
X	O	X	O						
X	O	X							
X	O								
X									

as with double and triple tops and bottoms, or in dynamic form, as with trend lines and triangles.

Point-and-Figure Price Targets

While entries into p&f chart pattern breaks are relatively easy to grasp for most bar and candlesticks traders, finding price targets on p&f charts is unique to this type of chart analysis. There are several different methods for finding price objectives on p&f

EXHIBIT 12.9

Bearish Breakdown below Symmetrical Triangle

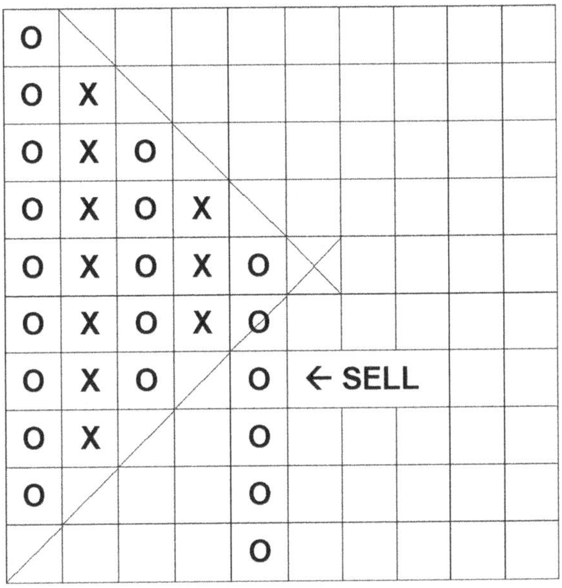

O								
O	X							
O	X	O						
O	X	O	X					
O	X	O	X	O				
O	X	O	X	O				
O	X	O		O	← SELL			
O	X			O				
O				O				
				O				

trades. Perhaps the most popular method for three-point reversal p&f charts is called the vertical count. The procedure for identifying the price objective on a vertical count is very simple. For targets on buy signals, the number of X boxes in the column in which the buy signal occurred would be multiplied by 3. Then the resulting product would be added to the same column's lowest box price. The sum would be the upside price objective. Similarly, for price targets on signals to sell short, the number of O boxes in the column in which the sell signal occurred would

189

be multiplied by 3. (Many p&f traders use 2 instead of 3 as a multiplier on short sells.) Then the resulting product would be subtracted from the same column's highest box price. The difference would be the downside price objective.

Point-and-figure charting is a solid, time-tested methodology for trading all of the major financial markets. Relying exclusively on price action concepts, p&f trading offers a clean and simple approach that lends clarity to any market.

Summary

This chapter introduced a lesser-known form of charting, point and figure. Although point-and-figure charting has significantly fewer adherents than bar or candlestick charting, it has proven itself over a long history to be one of the primary and standard tools of technical analysis.

The look and feel of point-and-figure charts is a radical departure for those that are used to using Open-High-Low-Close bar or candlestick charts. Very importantly, the element of time is excluded entirely on p&f charts, as is volume (for those markets that have available volume figures). For this reason, many traders consider p&f trading to be based purely on price action, as that is the only element that is focused on. P&f charts add an X or an O only if price actually makes a large enough move to fulfill the predetermined box size. Besides box size, reversal amount is also a variable that can be adjusted according to the particular market and trader/investor. These variables are instrumental in eliminating much of the market noise that is commonplace on bar and candlestick charts.

Summary

Many patterns can be found on p&f charts that aid in identifying the most prevalent trading opportunities: price breakouts. These include double-top/bottom breakouts, triple-top/bottom breakouts, trend line breakouts, and triangle breakouts. P&f charts also provide a unique, built-in methodology for identifying appropriate price targets.

CHAPTER 13

Volume

After reading this chapter, you will be able to:

- Know what role volume plays in augmenting the study of price action.
- Apply the study of trading volume to specific financial markets, especially the equities (stock) market.
- Understand the basics of the on-balance volume indicator.
- Realize that tick volume can be a lesser substitute for traditional volume in markets that do not have readily available, market-wide volume figures.

Introduction to Volume

Although volume is often a vital component of many traders' strategies and analyses, it will be discussed only in this one chapter because volume is far outweighed by price in the eyes of most technical analysts. As mentioned earlier, understanding price action is the key to understanding the bulk of technical analysis methods. While volume is often considered to be a leading indicator, it is generally used by the vast majority of traders and investors as a price-confirming indicator, albeit one of the most important ones. Furthermore, some markets, as in the futures and foreign exchange (forex) arenas, tend not to have volume figures available. Therefore, volume is primarily an indicator for the equities (stock) market.

Within the equities market, volume is simply the amount of a security's shares that are traded in a given period. Like other confirming indicators, volume is usually found right underneath the price chart, providing graphically represented numerical values for each price bar or candle on the chart. So, for example, on an hourly bar chart where each bar is worth one hour of price action, volume shows up underneath the price chart, displaying the amount of shares or contracts traded during each hour.

The key idea behind volume is that if it accompanies certain price moves or technical chart patterns, the likelihood that the actual result of the price move is the expected result becomes significantly greater. For example, in a typical head-and-shoulders top pattern, here are the ideal volume conditions:

- **Left shoulder.** Typically the highest volume within the pattern, higher than the head or the right shoulder. Volume increases on the incline and at the peak and decreases on the decline.

- **Head.** Although price reaches higher on the head than on the left shoulder, volume on the head is ideally less than on the left shoulder. As with the left shoulder, however, volume increases on the incline and decreases on the decline.

- **Right shoulder.** The price peak on the right shoulder is lower than the head, and the volume of the right shoulder should be significantly less than both the left shoulder and the head. Like both the left shoulder and the head, however, volume increases on the incline and decreases on the decline. The neckline should be at the end of the right shoulder decline. A breakdown of the neckline is the most important event in the life of a head-and-shoulders pattern, as it triggers the trade and confirms the topping pattern. Ideally, volume should be high on a neckline break.

Although a head-and-shoulders pattern can certainly be traded on price action alone without confirmation by volume, having those volume figures available lends strength and confirmation to the trading decision.

Besides the more elaborate examples, as shown with the head-and-shoulders pattern, one of the key concepts behind volume has to do with trends. Within a clear, established uptrend, volume should increase on bullish (up) moves in the direction of the trend and decrease on bearish (down) moves that are countertrend corrections. Likewise, within a clear, established downtrend, volume should increase on bearish (down) moves in the direction of the trend and decrease on bullish (up) moves that are countertrend corrections.

These ideal volume conditions are logical. In an uptrend, where bullish sentiment dominates, there is significantly increased investor participation, trading activity, and, therefore, volume on rising prices than on falling prices. In a downtrend, where bearish sentiment dominates, there is significantly increased investor participation, trading activity, and, therefore, volume on falling prices than on rising prices.

If these ideal volume conditions are not present, it can serve as a warning of a potential impending reversal. For example, if volume decreases on a bullish move within an uptrend, it could be a sign of a potential bearish reversal ahead. Likewise, if volume decreases on a bearish move within a downtrend, it could be a sign of a potential bullish reversal ahead. Similarly, during an uptrend, if there is increasing volume during a bearish retracement move or sideways consolidation, this could be an indication of a potential impending bearish reversal. And during a downtrend, if there is increasing volume during a bullish retracement move or sideways consolidation, this could be an indication of a potential impending bullish reversal.

Besides within the context of trends, volume is also a key confirming indicator for potential breakout trades. As in the example of the head-and-shoulders pattern provided earlier, where high trading volume is expected on the break of the pattern's neckline, other types of breakouts also tend to be more true and have more directional follow-through when they are accompanied by high volume. A breakout above a resistance level or a breakdown below a support level is all the more credible and actionable if it can be demonstrated that substantially increased trader participation accompanied the move. Volume is the indicator that can demonstrate this.

On-Balance Volume

Aside from the simple volume indicator that indicates the amount of shares traded during a given period, there is also another important volume indicator that goes a step further. It is called on-balance volume, or OBV. Introduced and popularized by Joseph Granville in his 1963 book, *Granville's New Key to Stock Market Profits*, OBV connects volume and price to provide a unique picture of both the leading and confirming nature of volume. OBV provides a cumulative total of volume and generally appears as a single moving line underneath the price bars, much like many other indicators or oscillators. To this cumulative total, the volume from a price period that closes higher than the previous price period is added and the volume from a price period that closes lower than the previous price period is subtracted. The OBV line moves up or down according to this addition or subtraction.

The key concept behind OBV is based on the principle mentioned earlier in this chapter regarding volume within the context of trends. During uptrends, volume should normally be higher and increasing on bullish moves (where a price period's close is higher than the previous price period). During downtrends, volume should normally be higher and increasing on bearish moves (where a price period's close is lower than the previous price period).

The OBV indicator is often used to identify divergences, much like the price-oscillator divergence signals that were discussed in Chapter 10. For example, if price in an uptrend makes a higher high but OBV only makes a lower high, the divergence displays a lack of volume participation in the price high and therefore a potential loss of continued upward momentum. This could be an early indication of a potential bearish price reversal. If price in a downtrend makes a lower low but OBV only makes a higher low, the divergence displays a lack of volume participation in the price low and therefore a potential loss of continued downward momentum. This could be an early indication of a potential bullish price reversal.

Tick Volume

Some markets do not have volume figures available, as mentioned previously. For example, the vast spot forex market generally does not have volume figures because there is a lack of a centralized exchange. Therefore, technical forex traders are left to analyze price action alone, or in conjunction with price-derived indicators and oscillators. In the absence of reliable trading volume figures, however, many of these traders have turned to using tick volume as a confirming indicator. Many charting platforms include this data and represent it below the price bars much like the actual trading volume indicator. Tick volume simply provides the number of ticks, or price movements, that occur within a given time period. So on an hourly chart, for example, below each hour-long price bar would be a visual representation of the number of ticks that occurred in that hour. Tick volume is certainly not the same as real trading volume but can be used as a lesser substitute. Especially in the case of a price breakout scenario, faster price movement (manifested as a higher tick volume) can certainly be used as a significant confirming indicator for the move.

Although price is always considered by technical analysts to be the most important aspect of any financial market, volume can be a very significant component of good decision making. Confirmation, whether with volume or with other technical indicators, is one of the keys to high-probability technical trading. This becomes more apparent in Chapter 14, which discusses technical trading strategies.

Summary

This chapter introduced the concept of trading volume. When volume information is available in a financial market, it can be used effectively to confirm price action moves. Generally speaking, under normal conditions, price moves in the direction of the prevailing trend should be accompanied by increased volume, while price moves against the prevailing trend should be accompanied by decreased volume. If this is not the case, then it could be an early sign that the trend may be weakening or even beginning to reverse. Likewise, technical traders prefer to see high volume accompanying a breakout of support or resistance in order for there to be greater confidence that the break is real.

On-balance volume is a volume indicator that goes a step further than the simple volume indicator by providing a cumulative running total of volume. OBV generally appears as a single moving line underneath the price bars, much like other indicators or oscillators. It is often used to identify divergence signals.

For those markets that do not have trading volume figures available, like the spot foreign exchange market, tick volume can be used as a lesser substitute. Tick volume is the number of ticks, or price movements, that occur within each given time period. High tick volume can be used for confirming price breakout moves.

CHAPTER 14

Technical Trading Strategies
Practical Applications

After reading this chapter, you will be able to:

- Appreciate some of the many methods and strategies commonly used by experienced technical traders.
- Comprehend the logic and reasoning behind some of the most widely used technical trading strategies.
- Apply and test high-probability trading strategies using specific strategy descriptions.
- Understand some of the key differences between manual and automated trading strategies.

Introduction to Technical Trading Strategies

This chapter melds together elements from all of the previous chapters to move toward the primary purpose of technical analysis: creating effective strategies to trade financial markets. With all of the essentials of technical analysis discussed thus far, the tools for formulating and implementing high-probability technical trading strategies are already present. All that needs to be done is to connect all of the pieces. This chapter helps do just that by introducing and describing several major technical trading strategies. These strategies are employed by traders and investors around the world who are involved in many different global financial markets.

Whenever any discussion of technical trading strategies takes place, it is always beneficial to make a distinction between manually traded strategies and automated strategies. Manually traded strategies often include those that involve a subjective, discretionary component on the part of the trader and therefore can only be traded manually by the human trader. Automated trading strategies are generally those that are completely mechanical and objective in their preprogrammed decision process and therefore can be traded entirely by computer trading platforms, without human assistance or interference. Both types of technical trading strategies, manual and automated, are discussed here. Where appropriate, the text specifies whether the strategy can generally only be traded manually due to a discretionary component or if the strategy can be traded both manually and on an automated basis.

The discussion of trading strategies progresses from the simplest, single-dimensional strategies all the way up to the more complex, multifaceted strategies. In all of technical analysis, there is perhaps no simpler an indicator than the moving average and no simpler a trading strategy than the moving average crossover.

Moving Average Crossovers

As touched on in Chapter 9, moving average crossovers can be of several different varieties. The simplest variety is price crossing one moving average, as shown in Exhibit 14.1. This is related to breakout trading, which is discussed in detail later in this chapter. The rules are

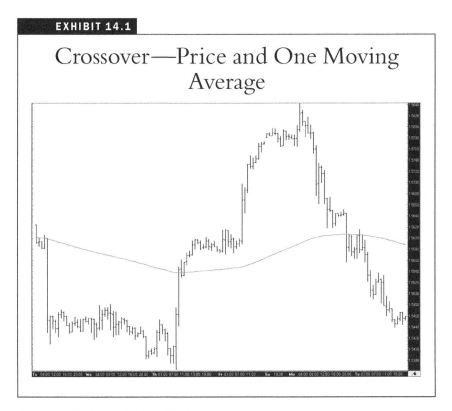

EXHIBIT 14.1

Crossover—Price and One Moving Average

Source: FX Solutions—FX AccuCharts

straightforward and objective enough to be a candidate for automated trading as well as manual trading. When price crosses above a certain moving average, that is a signal to buy, or go long. Conversely, when price crosses below that same moving average, that is a signal to sell short. The moving average periods that are commonly used, as well as the type (simple, exponential, weighted, or other), vary greatly. Generally speaking, when shorter-period moving averages are used for this type of a strategy, crossovers occur earlier and more often. When longer-period moving averages are used, crossovers occur later and less often. This give-and-take situation requires experimentation on the part of the trader to find the optimal period of moving average for the specific market and time frame in question.

A second type of moving average crossover, as shown in Exhibit 14.2, is probably the most commonly used moving average strategy, especially for novice traders. It involves the use of two moving averages of different periods. If the shorter-period moving average crosses above the longer one, it would be considered a signal to buy. Conversely, if the shorter-period moving average crosses below the longer one, it would be considered a signal to sell.

This strategy is widely used by many traders in all financial markets. It can be extremely effective in capturing a strong, prolonged trend relatively early in the trend's life cycle. The problem with this strategy, and really with all moving average strategies, however, occurs during markets that chop up and down, without any clear directional bias. During these market conditions, many moving average crosses that fail to follow through can occur in quick succession. In these instances, the many small losses incurred from this kind of whipsaw price action can quickly erode a trading account.

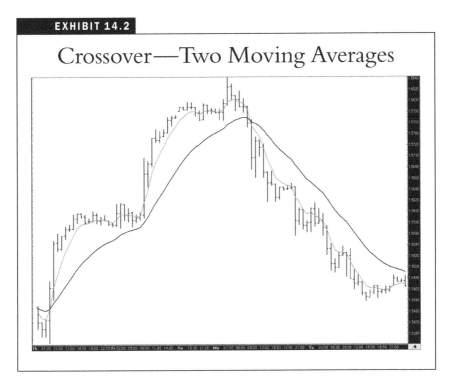

EXHIBIT 14.2

Crossover—Two Moving Averages

Source: FX Solutions—FX AccuCharts

Since these market conditions are inevitable, it is imperative that when a true cross with follow-through occurs, it should not be missed. The substantial profits of a good crossover trade are needed to offset all of the unprofitable sideways trades. Therefore, traders who employ crossover strategies generally tend to take all crossover opportunities that are presented by the market. Most crossover strategies using two moving averages are always in the market, whether long or short. Traders who employ these strategies cannot afford to miss any potentially lucrative trading opportunities.

The third essential type of moving average crossover, as shown in Exhibit 14.3, involves the use of three moving averages. This method

EXHIBIT 14.3

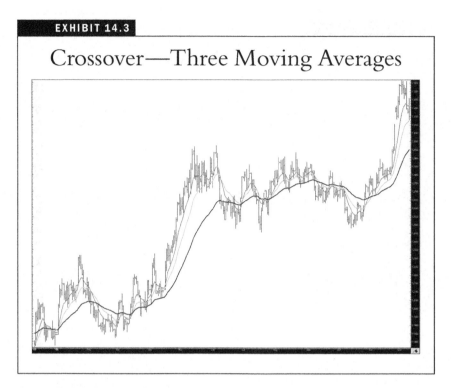

Crossover—Three Moving Averages

Source: FX Solutions—FX AccuCharts

of using multiple confirming lines attempts to help combat the unprofitable whipsaw price action just discussed that often results from sideways, nontrending markets. Strategies using three different moving averages usually produce signals when the shortest moving average crosses both longer moving averages or when the shortest moving average crosses the middle one and the middle one subsequently crosses the longest one.

As mentioned earlier, most moving average crossover strategies are generally always in the market. This means that after each trade is opened on a crossover and closed on an opposite crossover, another trade is immediately opened in the opposite direction to take the place of the previous trade. Therefore, there is always at least one trade open, whether long or short, depending on the prevailing crossover signal.

Also as mentioned earlier, traders should be aware that although crossover signals can often be exceptionally profitable, those traders who use them must be prepared for frequent losses resulting from common whipsaw price action. Whipsaws can occur regardless of however many moving averages and confirmation crossovers happen to be utilized in any given trading strategy. The most common whipsaws happen when crossovers occur incessantly because of non-trending, sideways price action, as shown in Exhibit 14.4. This type

EXHIBIT 14.4

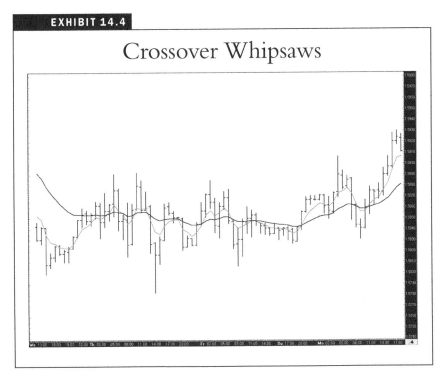

Source: FX Solutions—FX AccuCharts

of choppiness almost always results in multiple false crossover signals with little to no follow-through, and consequently a string of many small losses. Whipsaws are an unavoidable fact of trading with moving averages.

The concept behind successful moving average trading methods, as alluded to earlier, centers on the goal of gaining large profits during trending periods when crossovers are few and far between while at the same time withstanding the inevitable small losses during sideways whipsaw periods when crossovers are abundant. The greatest challenge with this type of trading lies in the ability of the trader to let the winning trades run while immediately closing losing trades. Only in this way can a trader using moving averages profit enough during trends to offset the many losses typically incurred during horizontal price activity and eventually come out ahead.

Exiting out of moving average crossover trades is usually as simple as waiting for a cross back in the opposite direction from the entry. Likewise, entering into moving average crossover trades can be just as simple as waiting for the cross to occur and then executing the appropriate trade. Many crossover traders, however, will add an entry filter to delay getting into a trade. The purpose of an entry filter is to seek additional confirmation that both a crossover and a bona fide directional move has taken place. One example of an entry filter is to wait until the market moves a minimum price increment in the direction of the trade after the crossover takes place. This provides some additional confirmation that momentum may indeed be in the direction of the intended trade. Another example of an entry filter is to wait until another indicator or oscillator points in the direction of the trade after the moving average crossover occurs. Again, this provides some additional confirmation that momentum may in fact be on the side of the potential trade.

Besides moving average crossovers, another popular crossover strategy involves the use of components of the average directional index (ADX) indicator, developed by J. Welles Wilder, as mentioned in Chapter 10. The ADX itself is a trend strength indicator. Its components include the positive directional indicator (DI+) and the negative directional indicator (DI−), which are directional indications that, when put together, measure trend strength in the form of the ADX. When viewed on a chart, it can clearly be seen that a cross of the DI+ above the DI− can be considered a signal to buy the market, while a cross of the DI− above the DI+ can be considered a signal to sell the market. As with moving averages, however, the primary caveat when using DI+ and DI− in a crossover strategy is that unprofitable whipsaws (when crossovers occur incessantly due to choppy, sideways price action) can take place frequently in all financial markets.

IN THE REAL WORLD

Confluence

The vitally important concept of confluence within the realm of technical trading may mean different things to different traders. The basic idea, however, is that multiple technical confirmations make for a stronger trade rationale and therefore a higher-probability trade. Confluence is simply more than one technical indication providing a basis for any given trading action. This could be any combination of two or more technical factors pointing in the same direction. Some examples of these technical

IN THE REAL WORLD (CONTINUED)

include support/resistance levels, trend lines, Fibonacci levels, pivot points, Western bar patterns, Japanese candlestick patterns, moving averages, and volatility bands.

It should be noted that seeking confluence for a given trade should not be an exercise in paralysis by analysis, where all stars need to be perfectly aligned before the afflicted trader can pull the trigger on the trade. Paralysis by analysis can be a debilitating condition that hinders traders from making otherwise good trading decisions. Rather, seeking confluence is simply the act of finding some additional, reasonable confirmation(s) for reinforcing the rationale for a trade. This is a key component of high-probability technical trading and analysis.

Patience is of the utmost importance when seeking to trade with confluence. This is due to the fact that potential trades with only one rationale are far more plentiful than those setups that have a confluence of more than one rationale. If one has the patience to wait for confluence to develop before taking any trades, however, the success probability for those fewer, select trades increases significantly. Patience is important when waiting for confluence to develop also because the confirmations are not always simultaneous. Rather, confluence can often develop in a consecutive manner. For example, in a breakout confluence where price breaks out above a certain horizontal price resistance level, a confirming breakout above a separate downtrend resistance trend line may occur a few bars (periods) later. But this breakout could still be considered a potential trade setup with confluence, even though the confirming break occurred after the initial break instead of simultaneously.

Some common examples of potential trade setups that can be considered to have a confluence of technical factors are presented next.

- Bounce up off a horizontal support level coinciding with an uptrend support line
- Bounce up off a 38.2 percent Fibonacci level coinciding with both a daily S1 pivot point and a horizontal support level
- Bounce down off a long-term 61.8 percent Fibonacci level coinciding with a short-term 38.2 percent Fibonacci level
- Bounce down off a downtrend resistance line coinciding with both a horizontal resistance level and an R2 pivot point
- Breakdown below a major horizontal support level coinciding with a head-and-shoulders neckline
- Bounce up off a key moving average coinciding with an uptrend support line
- Breakout above a pennant pattern coinciding with a major resistance level
- Bounce up off a newly formed bottom confirmed by a hammer candle coinciding with a major previous support level
- Bounces off Bollinger Bands' lower and upper standard deviation bands coinciding with strong horizontal support and resistance within a sideways trading range
- Bounce up off a clear support level coinciding with a relative strength index (RSI) emergence above oversold territory

These are only a few examples of the countless potential combinations of confluence factors that can be found on any financial market chart. Overall, confluence can be an extremely important contributing factor to fostering prudent, high-probability technical trading.

Breakout Trading

Aside from the countless variations of moving average crossovers and other crossover strategies, another type of strategy that is widely used both by novice traders as well as by those that are more experienced is breakout trading. The entire concept behind trading breakouts is based on price violations of support and resistance. This key concept of support and resistance is central to the entire field of technical analysis and was described in detail in Chapter 6.

The theory behind breakout trading is that, under normal circumstances, support and resistance levels should be respected. This is the psychological norm of financial markets. If a strong enough catalyst exists to violate a support or resistance level in any significant manner, that catalyst should theoretically be strong enough to further propel price in the direction of the breakout, thereby rewarding those traders who participated in that breakout opportunity. Of course, this happy circumstance is not always to be the case. In fact, the preponderance of false breakouts, where price breaks a support or resistance level and then turns back around and moves in the opposite direction, thereby trapping all of those who hastily jumped on the opportunity, has been the bane of breakout traders since the early days of technical trading.

False breakouts notwithstanding, the logic behind breakout trading is sound. With good risk management in place, it can be a high-probability approach to trading financial markets.

When discussing breakout trading strategies, it should be recalled that there are two primary types of support and resistance: static and dynamic. Static support and resistance are in the form of horizontal lines, where the price level does not change over time. Static support and resistance can stem from levels where price turned or reversed in the past. Dynamic support and resistance are in the form of angled trend lines, where, for example, uptrend lines provide support that is progressively higher in price over time while downtrend lines provide resistance that is progressively lower in price over time. Breakout trading opportunities can be found on price violations of any of these types of support or resistance.

For example, as shown in Exhibit 14.5, if there is a certain price level to the upside where price has turned back down several times in the past, that level can be considered an established resistance level. If

EXHIBIT 14.5

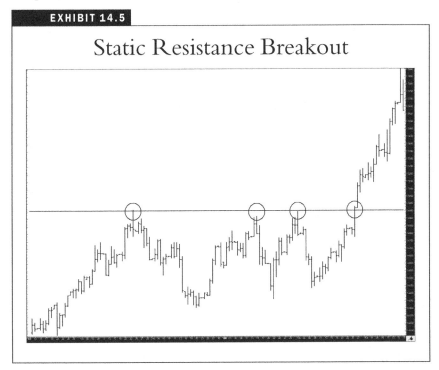

Static Resistance Breakout

Source: FX Solutions—FX AccuCharts

price approaches that level again, the expectation would be that price would turn back down once again, as that level has been considered by market participants to be relatively high, and selling pressure should therefore overcome buying pressure around that level. If, however, a strong enough catalyst exists in the market to push price beyond that established resistance level, the momentum in the direction of the breakout could potentially be strong enough to propel price to the next further resistance level to the upside. This type of follow-through provides substantial profits for breakout traders.

Exhibit 14.6 shows the same principle, but to the downside. A price breakdown of an established support level can represent a strong

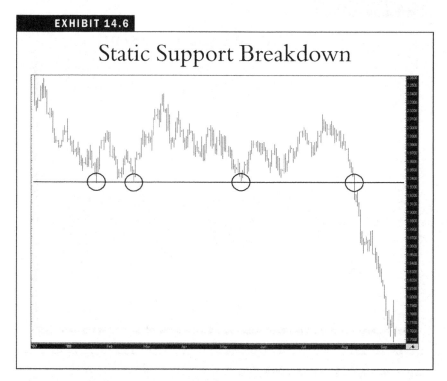

EXHIBIT 14.6

Static Support Breakdown

Source: FX Solutions—FX AccuCharts

EXHIBIT 14.7

Dynamic Resistance Breakout

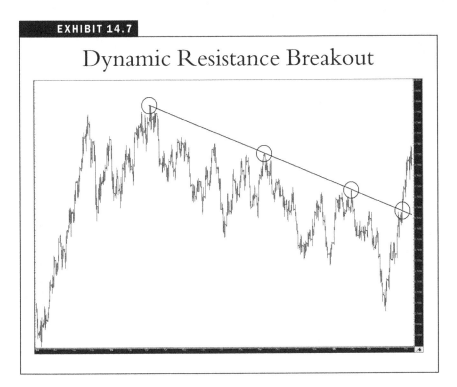

Source: FX Solutions—FX AccuCharts

reason to sell a market short. When this occurs, the expectation is that price continues to the downside after the break, providing the follow-through that is so sought after by traders who participate in breakouts.

A dynamic resistance breakout, as shown in Exhibit 14.7, occurs when an established downtrend resistance line is broken to the upside. This breakout event is an indication of a potential trend reversal where the prevailing downtrend can possibly turn into a new uptrend. When downtrend resistance lines of this nature are broken, the assumption is that some significant catalyst has interrupted the

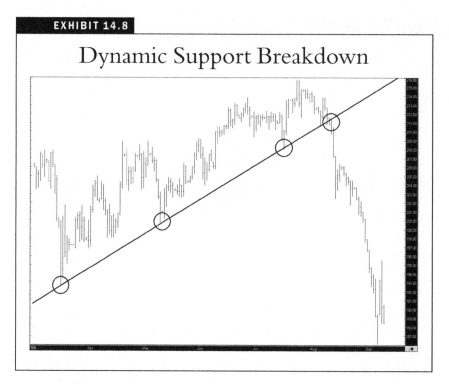

EXHIBIT 14.8

Dynamic Support Breakdown

Source: FX Solutions—FX AccuCharts

normal flow of the downtrend, and a substantial move to the upside could potentially be the result.

Likewise, as shown in Exhibit 14.8, a dynamic support breakdown is characterized by a price breakdown below an established uptrend support line. This breakout event is an indication of a potential trend reversal where the prevailing uptrend can possibly turn into a new downtrend. When uptrend support lines of this nature are broken, the assumption is that some significant catalyst has interrupted the normal flow of the uptrend, and a substantial move to the downside could potentially be the result.

Besides breakdowns of uptrend lines and downtrend lines, another form of dynamic breakout is the chart pattern breakout. Most chart pattern breakouts can be considered volatility breakouts, where the low-volatility consolidation of a chart pattern breaks out into higher volatility and momentum. The primary and most relevant Western chart patterns were described in detail in Chapter 8. The borders of all these Western chart patterns represent dynamic support or resistance, and they all require some kind of a dynamic break in order to initiate trading action. For example, a triangle requires a break of either its upper or lower angled border in order for the trader to be justified in initiating a long or short trade out of the consolidation. Likewise, flag patterns, pennant patterns, wedges, and rectangles all need for price to break out of their formations before any meaningful trading action should take place. As for reversal patterns, the situation is similar. For example, price should break down below the previously established trough of a double-top reversal in order for a short (sell) trade to be reasonably initiated. By the same token, price should break down below the neckline of a head-and-shoulders reversal pattern before a short trade would be justified. Western chart patterns represent extremely common instances of dynamic breakout opportunities in all financial markets.

To many traders, breakout trading makes more sense than other methods of trading, as a breakout with strong momentum can potentially yield a high profit for a considerably smaller amount of risk. For this reason, many traders gravitate immediately to trading breakouts. While it is true that breakout trading can offer a high-probability method of approaching technical trading, the preponderance of false breakouts, as mentioned earlier, necessitates paying close attention to strict risk management practices when executing breakout trades.

These risk management practices, first and foremost, revolve around proper stop-loss strategy. The extensive and important topic of risk management is discussed in detail in Chapter 15, but a simple stop-loss strategy for breakout trades is described here. The goal of any sound technical analysis–based stop-loss strategy should revolve around the point at which one's analysis is proven by the market to be wrong. When this is the case, the trade that was proven to be wrong should be terminated immediately through the use of a hard stop-loss. This ensures that funds are preserved if the market moves against one's position.

In breakout trading situations, the market proves one's analysis wrong when price fails to show follow-through and instead reverts to a point before the false or premature breakout occurred. Where exactly is this point? Theoretically, the reasons for getting into a breakout trade are proven wrong as soon as price returns to any point before the breakout. So, for example, as shown in Exhibit 14.9, if price broke above the resistance line and then subsequently dipped back below the line, the trade should be invalidated immediately. Practically, however, there are many instances of price action moving slightly above and below an important breakout level before eventually continuing in the direction of the original breakout. Therefore, a stop-loss strategy that allows for more breathing room entails placing the stop-loss right under the last minor dip in an upside resistance breakout scenario or right above the last minor rally in a downside support breakdown scenario. This strategy provides a strict market-driven stop-loss while also giving a trade the necessary room to develop.

EXHIBIT 14.9

Breakout Trading Risk Management

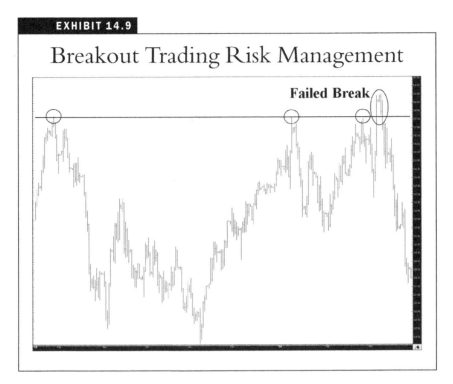

Source: FX Solutions—FX AccuCharts

Much as with the moving average crossovers discussed earlier in this chapter, breakout traders also utilize entry filters to help confirm that a potentially tradable event may indeed be in the making. Similar to waiting for a certain minimum price increment after a moving average crossover before getting into the trade, breakout traders often also wait for a certain minimum price increment beyond the breakout level before committing to a trade. If price is able to move that minimum price increment beyond the break, there is a stronger argument that momentum may indeed be in the direction of the breakout.

Another entry filter for breakout traders occurs after the bar or candlestick that breaks the support or resistance level closes. Once a breakout occurs, the trader would wait for the breakout bar to close. If the bar does not close beyond the breakout level, it is not yet considered a true breakout. If the close does occur beyond the breakout, the trader would wait for the next bar to surpass the breakout bar's extreme (in the direction of the breakout) before actually getting into the trade. If the next bar fails to surpass the breakout bar's extreme, the trader simply waits for subsequent bars to do so. Like the minimum price increment filter, this entry filter helps to avoid commitment to many false breakout scenarios.

Yet another entry filter, one that excels in its common use as a secondary entry into a breakout opportunity, is the pullback/throwback. Pullbacks and throwbacks, as illustrated in Exhibit 14.10, occur

EXHIBIT 14.10

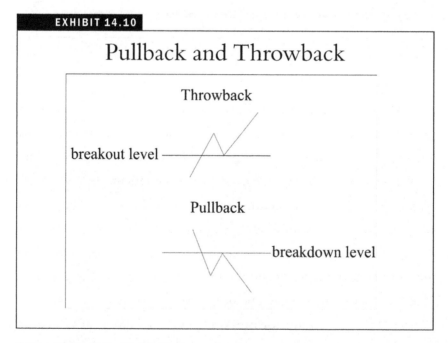

Pullback and Throwback

Source: FX Solutions—FX AccuCharts

when momentum on a breakout wanes shortly after the break, resulting in an extra move that often retests the point of breakout. To differentiate the two terms, a throwback is simply a return to, or retest of, the point of breakout after an upward break. Conversely, a pullback is a return to, or retest of, the point of breakdown after a downward break. In either direction, if the break is true (which means it carries real directional momentum), price should hit and bounce off the point of breakout and then surpass the point at which breakout momentum waned and price turned. On a true break, price should then continue in the breakout direction as if the pullback or throwback never occurred. Some breakout traders will wait for a pullback/throwback before getting in on a breakout trade. Others will use pullbacks/throwbacks as secondary breakout entries if the first entry was missed. In either case, the point of entry should be where price surpasses the high after breakout in an upside breakout scenario or the low after breakdown in a downside breakout scenario.

Generally, breakout trading can be a high-probability approach to analyzing and trading any financial market, as breakouts of support/resistance, whether static or dynamic, are very commonplace in all markets. Solid risk management practices, however, need to be in place to ensure that the potential pitfalls of breakout trading, namely false breakouts, are kept in proper check.

Using prudent stop-loss placement to exit a breakout trade and minimize losses if the market proves the trade to be wrong was discussed earlier in this chapter. As for exits when in profit, one common method involves the use of further support/resistance levels, whether static or dynamic, as profit target zones. In an upside breakout above an established resistance line, for example, a further resistance target above can be used to close the entire trade, or a portion of the entire trade, in profit. Another profit exit strategy involves the use of a trailing stop-loss methodology. This is discussed in Chapter 15, on risk management.

Besides static horizontal lines, dynamic angled trend lines, and Western chart patterns, other chart elements can also create breakout trading opportunities. These include moving averages (e.g., price crossing over one moving average), volatility bands (e.g., Bollinger Bands), pivot points, Fibonacci retracement lines, and many others.

One notable form of breakout trading utilizing the popular Bollinger Bands was introduced in Chapter 10. This method is a form of volatility breakout trading that exploits the well-observed tendency for periods of high volatility in financial markets to follow periods of low volatility. Low volatility on the Bollinger Bands is represented by a tightening or a narrowing of the bands. This is called the *squeeze*. The anticipated event after this period of low market volatility is a sudden, sharp increase in volatility, which often manifests itself as a directional breakout move. Thus, traders may take advantage of this burst of volatility by jumping on a trade once price breaks away from the Bollinger Bands' squeeze.

As for automated trading, some types of breakout strategies can certainly be automated to be traded by computers alone. For example, a strategy that can be automated might give the instructions to buy if the high of the last 20 days is broken to the upside or to sell if the low of the last 20 days is broken to the downside. For many forms of breakout trading, however, there are too many discretionary components to automate effectively. For example, trend line analysis is, by nature, highly subjective and therefore difficult to automate. Many applications of successful breakout trading require the judgment and discretion of an experienced trader.

IN THE REAL WORLD

"Turtles" Trading

In the early 1980s, a well-known commodities trader by the name of Richard Dennis gathered a group of individuals and trained them to trade commodities using his specific trend-following methodology. This came about because Dennis intended to prove to his friend, another trader by the name of William Eckhardt, that good traders were made, not born. The individuals recruited for this experiment were attracted to the opportunity by major newspaper ads. The final group was narrowed down through interviews with Dennis, and the ones who made the cut were eventually dubbed the Turtles. This was due to the fact that Dennis had just returned from Singapore, and he wished to "grow traders just like they grow turtles."

The set of trend-following trading rules that Dennis taught the Turtles are now widely known. Back in the 1980s, these rules helped the Turtles earn over $100 million in trading profits as a group. The trading rules, which were based largely on Richard Donchian's channel breakout methods, are generally simple and easy to follow. One of the primary differentiators between those Turtles who were successful and those who were not as successful was the ability to follow these rules to the letter, without emotions or individual biases. In a nutshell, the entry rules, at their most basic level, are described by the next two sets of general system guidelines.

- **System #1 (shorter term).** Enter a long position on a breakout above the price high of the preceding 20 days, or enter a short position on a breakdown below the price low

In the Real World (continued)

of the preceding 20 days. If the most recent breakout was a true breakout that resulted in a winning trade, any current breakout entry signal would be ignored. If the most recent breakout was a false breakout (i.e., one that moved against the position by a certain predetermined amount after the breakout signal was given), the current breakout signal could be taken. If a breakout signal is not taken due to a winning trade on the most recent breakout, a trade would be taken anyway on a 55-day breakout signal to capture any major price moves.

- **System #2 (longer term).** Enter a long position on a breakout above the high of the preceding 55 days, or enter a short position on a breakdown below the low of the preceding 55 days. Unlike System #1, regardless of whether the most recent breakout was a winning trade or a losing trade, all breakout signals are taken.

Trend Trading

Like breakout trading, trend trading, or trend following, is another class of market strategy that claims a large number of practitioners. The comprehensive concept of trend was described in detail in Chapter 5. There are many ways to trade a trend, all of which entail exploiting the natural directional bias of a given financial market. Not only is the direction important, however, but the timing and location of the trade entry are also vital to an advantageous trade.

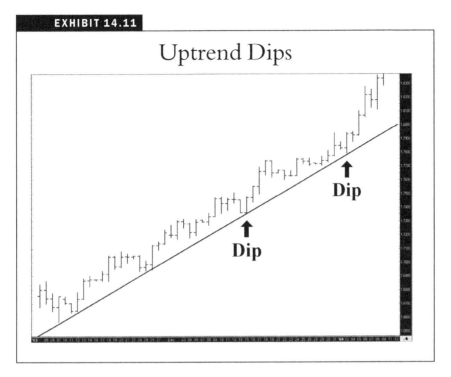

EXHIBIT 14.11

Uptrend Dips

Source: FX Solutions—FX AccuCharts

This often means entering trends on countertrend retracements, more commonly known as dips in an uptrend (Exhibit 14.11) and rallies in a downtrend (Exhibit 14.12). Within an uptrend situation, the expectation is that the upward bias should continue in the absence of any strong catalysts that would reverse the uptrend. The most advantageous price location to get into an uptrend of this nature is to buy at as low a price as possible to maximize future potential profits when ultimately selling the position. Similarly, within a downtrend situation, the expectation is that the downward bias should continue in the absence of any strong catalysts that would reverse the downtrend. The most advantageous price location to get into a

EXHIBIT 14.12

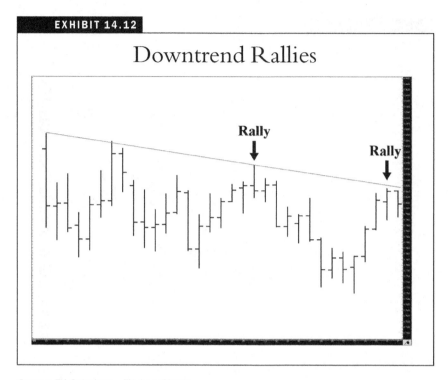

Downtrend Rallies

Source: FX Solutions—FX AccuCharts

downtrend of this nature is to sell short at as high a price as possible to maximize future potential profits when ultimately covering (buying back) the position.

Two essential tools for identifying dips in uptrends and rallies in downtrends are trend lines and moving averages. For both of these tools, the trend trader is looking for price to respect, or bounce off, the trend line or moving average. In this respect, trend trading a trend line is the polar opposite of trading trend line breakouts, and trend trading a moving average is the polar opposite of trading moving average breakouts.

Trend lines were introduced and described in Chapter 7. Trend trading with a trend line simply entails drawing a trend line to connect progressively higher lows in an uptrend or progressively lower highs in a downtrend and then trading the subsequent bounces, or near bounces, off the line. As mentioned in Chapter 7, the more price touches an uptrend support line or downtrend resistance line, the more valid the trend line tends to be.

Strategies for entering into a trend trade off a significant trend line bounce necessarily incorporate techniques for helping to confirm that a bounce has indeed occurred. These techniques fall under the same banner of entry filters as did very similar techniques described earlier for breakout trading. One common method involves waiting for price to bounce up off an uptrend support line or down off a downtrend resistance line by a certain minimum price increment before getting into a trend trade, much as one might do to filter out false breaks on a potential breakout trade. Waiting for a minimum price increment bounce in this manner helps to confirm that price may indeed have some momentum on the bounce.

Another entry filter technique involves close observation of the "bounce bar." The bounce bar is the bar that actually bounces off the trend line (or comes close to it), whether it is a bounce up off uptrend support or a bounce down off downtrend resistance. Once the bounce bar closes on a bounce above an uptrend support line, for example, one would refrain from entering into a long trend trade unless or until the next bar, or subsequent bar(s), surpasses the high extreme of the bounce bar. This entry filter provides additional confirmation that a true bounce may indeed have taken place. For a downtrend resistance bounce, one would refrain from entering into a short trend trade unless or until the next bar, or subsequent bar(s), surpasses the low extreme of the bounce bar.

Yet another entry filter for trend trades entails trading counter-trend breakouts in the direction of the larger trend. This strategy is explained in detail in the Tips and Techniques section on "Trading with the Trend Using Countertrend Breakouts."

TIPS AND TECHNIQUES

Trading with the Trend Using Countertrend Breakouts

Trend trading using countertrend breakouts is a specific, high-probability method for approaching a market that is in clear trending mode. The simple concept behind this approach is that the best entry into an existing trend occurs right after a retracement or consolidation in that trend begins to move in the direction of the trend once again. This is exactly the rationale for trading countertrend breakouts.

In an uptrend, for example, traders who are looking to enter long (buy) into the trend will always look for an optimal entry location. The best place to get in on an uptrend is a temporary dip in the market. When traders enter on a dip, they can get in at a "cheaper" price. Furthermore, any subsequent continuation of the trend provides these dip trades with increased profits due to the optimal location of entry. Similarly, in a downtrend situation, traders who are looking to enter short (sell) into the trend will also always seek an optimal entry location. The best place to get in on a downtrend is a temporary rally in the market.

The trend can be measured by a trend line, a parallel trend channel, a linear regression line, or even a moving average. Once one or more of these studies is in place, measuring and marking the full strength of the trend, attention can be turned to counter-trend trend lines.

Using the same example of an uptrending situation, which is marked by an uptrend support line (connecting the lows of the uptrend), when price retraces, or dips, back to the uptrend line, it often creates a minor downtrend resistance line (connecting the highs of the minor downtrend) that runs counter to the prevailing uptrend. When this occurs, the strategy that can be implemented after price reaches down and bounces up off the major uptrend support line is to trade any breakouts above the minor downtrend resistance line.

So in an uptrending situation that is confirmed by a strong uptrend support line, for example, traders would be looking for shorter-term downtrends that go against this trend. When one of these shorter-term downtrends appear, a downtrend resistance line can be drawn connecting the descending tops. If and when a significant breakout above one of these downtrend lines occurs, that is a potential signal to enter into a long trade, in the same direction as the prevailing trend.

Conversely, in an overall downtrending situation that is confirmed by a strong downtrend resistance line, for example, traders would be looking for shorter-term uptrends that go against this trend. When one of these shorter-term uptrends appears, an uptrend support line can be drawn connecting the ascending bottoms. If and when a significant break down below one of these uptrend lines occurs, that is a potential signal to enter into a short trade, in the same direction as the prevailing trend.

Trading countertrend breakouts in the direction of the trend is a solid, effective approach for getting in on and timing trend line bounces. Although this method may produce somewhat later entries than some other trend-trading methods, it is a high-probability method to provide additional confirmation that a trend line bounce could potentially carry substantial momentum and follow-through.

Similar to breakout trading are the stop-loss strategies and profit exits customarily used during trend trading. Stop-losses should follow the same principle as any other type of technical trading: A trend trade should be terminated immediately when the original reasons behind the trade are proven invalid. In the case of a trend line trade, a significant break of the trend line would invalidate the trade. Therefore, stop-losses following this principle would be placed on the other side of the trend line. In an uptrend, the stop-loss would be placed below the trend line, directly under the most recent dip in the market. In a downtrend, the stop-loss would be placed above the trend line, directly above the most recent rally in the market.

Profit exits can be based on support and resistance levels, or a trailing stop-loss methodology can be employed. This is discussed further in Chapter 15. Additionally, when price action can be framed within a parallel trend channel, whether up or down, built-in profit exits exist around what is called the return line. This concept was described in Chapter 7. In a parallel uptrend channel, the return line is the upper resistance line that acts as a dynamic profit target for long trades taken at or near the lower support line. In a parallel downtrend channel, the return line is the lower support line that acts as a dynamic profit target for short trades taken at or near the upper resistance line.

Because of the rather subjective nature of trend line drawing and analysis, it can be difficult, at best, to automate trend line trading strategies. If it is to be at its most effective, trend line trading requires the full human control and attention of the trader.

Less subjective in its trend trading process is the use of moving averages to identify dips in uptrends and rallies in downtrends, as shown in Exhibit 14.13. Moving averages, as described in Chapter 9,

EXHIBIT 14.13

Trend Trading with Moving Averages

Source: FX Solutions—FX AccuCharts

can be considered dynamic representations of the trend that are mathematically derived, unlike trend lines. Especially during strong and well-defined trends, moving averages of various periods often serve remarkably well as dynamic support for dips in an uptrend or dynamic resistance for rallies in a downtrend. These moving averages can be used both to enter into trend trades on those dips and rallies as well as to exit trend trades for profit at opportune price levels.

Entries into moving average trend trades follow the same general principles as entries into trend line trades. The period of the moving average chosen for any given trend should be experimented with until one that fits the current trend is found. Generally, the stronger the trend, the shorter the period of the moving average. Often there will not be any period that fits the prevailing trend well. In these cases, this particular trend trading strategy should not be used. If a moving average, whether simple, exponential, or other, fits the current trend well, dips to the moving average in an uptrend or rallies to the moving average in a downtrend can be traded in much the same way as with trend lines.

In terms of exits, much as with trend lines, initial stop-losses can be prudently placed under the previous dip in an uptrend or above the previous rally in a downtrend.

Profit exits on moving average trend trades can be straightforward. In an uptrend situation, on any simple price cross and close below the chosen moving average, the long trade can be closed for a profit. In a downtrend situation, on any simple price cross and close above the chosen moving average, the short trade can be closed for a profit. This method of exiting in profit represents a way of allowing the market to dictate the end of a directional price run.

This moving average method of trend trading is easier to automate than the trend line method. Some discretion, however, can often be helpful in determining entries for moving average trend trades.

EXECUTIVE INSIGHT

Dr. Alexander Elder, Triple Screen Trading System

In a written interview with the author, Dr. Alexander Elder, a psychiatrist, trader, and expert in both technical analysis and financial market psychology, explains the rationale for his famed Triple Screen trading system. Elder wrote, among other prominent books, the international bestselling classic *Trading for a Living* and the comprehensive trading tome *Come into My Trading Room: A Complete Guide to Trading*. He is the founder and director of Financial Trading, Inc., and Elder.com.

Elder states:

> Every tick in the financial markets reflects a transaction between a buyer and a seller. Individual decisions may be based on facts, but also to a large extent on emotion. The buyer believes that prices are headed higher—otherwise he'd wait to buy cheaper. The seller believes that prices are headed lower—had he thought otherwise, he'd wait to sell. This is why every tick represents a conflict between two individuals.
>
> Those single ticks coalesce into bars, be they on 5-minute, hourly, daily, weekly, or monthly charts. We must keep in mind that any chart reflects innumerable conflicts between buyers and sellers, winners, and losers. This is why technical analysis is the study of crowd behavior—it is applied social psychology.
>
> The trends of the same trading vehicle in different timeframes often contradict one another. A stock or a currency may be rising on a monthly chart, but falling on the weekly, or declining on the hourly chart but rallying on the 5-minute chart. Markets may move in different directions in different timeframes at the same time.
>
> The key tactic of Triple Screen trading system is to choose your favorite timeframe—but then not look at it. We must first open the chart in the timeframe one order of magnitude greater than the one we like to analyze. That is where we should make a strategic decision to go long or short. Afterwards we can return to our favorite timeframe and make tactical decisions about entries and exits, targets and stops.
>
> Adding the dimension of time to our analysis gives us an edge over the competition. Triple Screen allows us to take only those trades that have passed the filters of long-term and short-term charts. This action cuts out many trades that may have seemed attractive at first but are troublesome in another timeframe.

Triple Screen promotes a careful and cautious approach to trading.

The key principle of Triple Screen is to begin your analysis by stepping back from the markets and looking at the big picture for strategic decisions. Use a long-term chart to decide whether you are bullish or bearish, then return closer to the market and make tactical choices about entries and exits.

TIPS AND TECHNIQUES

Multiple Time Frame Trading

One of the highest-probability and most effective strategies for trading any major financial market is through a multiple time frame approach. This approach falls under the general category of trend following and therefore thrives in trending conditions while seeking to avoid sideways markets where unprofitable whipsaws prevail.

The specific method of multiple time frame trading described here is based largely on the Triple Screen methodology originated by Dr. Alexander Elder. Elder explains the rationale for his unique and time-tested methodology in the previous "Executive Insight" section. The particular multiple time frame approach described here follows the essential concepts of the Triple Screen but includes some minor technique modifications.

The key concept behind this multiple time frame approach is that a successful trader views the market from different angles in order to understand and apply the critical strategic components of (1) trend, (2) retracement, and (3) entry. The primary objective of multiple time frame trading is to enter into a strong trend at the most opportune time and price. This would be after a minor countertrend retracement ends and price subsequently resumes in the direction of the trend.

The process of implementing an effective multiple time frame strategy begins with a simple choice of which time frames to use. Three time frames should ultimately be chosen to execute the strategy. The best way to approach this choice is first to identify one's customarily preferred time frame and label it as the intermediate time frame. For example, if one is accustomed to trading most frequently on 1-hour (60-minute) charts, one would call that time frame intermediate.

To derive the longest-term time frame, one would take one's intermediate time frame and multiply it by 4 to 6. This range of multipliers provides flexibility for the trader to fine-tune the choice of time frames. As an example of the longest-term time frame, the aforementioned 1-hour chart trader might multiply by 4 to settle on the 4-hour (240-minute) chart as the time frame for the longest term.

Similarly, to derive the shortest-term time frame, one would simply take one's intermediate time frame and divide it by 4 to 6. To use the 1-hour trader as an example once again, that trader might divide the 1-hour (60-minute) chart by 6 to settle on the 10-minute chart as the ideal shortest-term time frame.

Once the three time frames are determined, the work of implementing this approach can begin. The long-term time frame represents the strategic element of trend. The sole function of this time frame is to determine the overall trend conditions—if the current market is trending up, trending down, or nontrending. If a certain market is determined to be nontrending, a decision should be made to refrain from trading that particular market at that particular time. If the market is determined to be trending up, only long trades should be taken. Conversely, if the market is determined to be trending down, only short trades should be taken.

TIPS AND TECHNIQUES (CONTINUED)

The trend can readily be determined through several subjective or objective methods. One of the subjective methods is to draw simple dynamic trend lines—primarily uptrend support or downtrend resistance. If a trend line can be drawn convincingly to connect higher lows in an uptrend or lower highs in a downtrend, there is good potential that a trend is indeed present. If not, that particular market should be avoided at that particular time.

Alternatively, for a more objective method, if all of the exponential moving averages in a multiple set (e.g., 10, 20, 30, 50, and 100 periods, or any combination the trader wishes to use) are in the correct order for an uptrend (shorter-period moving averages on top followed by progressively longer periods toward the bottom), price can be considered to be in an uptrend on a longer-term basis. Conversely, if all the moving averages are in the correct order for a downtrend (shorter-period moving averages on the bottom followed by progressively longer periods toward the top), price can be considered to be in a downtrend on a longer-term basis. Any situation where there is a lack of correct order would signify a market that is nontrending. In this event, trading should be avoided on that particular market at that particular time.

Once the presence and direction of the trend is determined on the longest time frame, the focus would then turn to the intermediate time frame. This time frame represents the strategic element of retracement, or correction. A minor dip in an uptrend or a minor rally in a downtrend represents an ideal location for getting in on high-probability, risk-controlled trades.

For this, an oscillator would be employed. Oscillators help confirm overbought and oversold conditions and give readings of overall price momentum. There are countless variations of oscillators available to traders, but only a handful are widely used. These include relative strength index (RSI), stochastics, rate of change (ROC), commodity channel index (CCI), and Williams %R, among a few others.

A multiple time frame trader viewing the intermediate time frame would scan for instances when the countertrend retracement move within the longer-term trend becomes exhausted. The method by which this exhaustion is measured relies on crosses of the oscillator over the horizontal lines of demarcation between the overbought/oversold regions and the middle region of the oscillator range. For example, on the stochastics oscillator, a move down from overbought (crossing below 80) would be a sell (short) signal within a long-term downtrend, while a move up from oversold (crossing above 20) would be a buy signal within a long-term uptrend.

Once the longest time frame is showing a significant trend and the intermediate time frame is indicating that price may be in the process of resuming the prevailing trend after a minor countertrend retracement, the final step is to drill down to the third, and shortest, time frame.

The sole purpose of this shortest time frame is to seek the most opportune entry point possible. This is accomplished by implementing a trailing entry stop strategy. At this point within the multiple time frame trading process, the trader has already been assured that a trend is indeed in place and that any trading will be in the direction of this primary trend. The trader also knows that a countertrend retracement within the trend has occurred and that price is in the process of recovering from this trend setback.

The only remaining consideration before committing to this trade is planning the actual execution of the entry. Using the trailing entry stop methodology, the trader wisely waits for price to come to him or her rather than chasing a runaway market.

A trailing entry stop as it relates to multiple time frame trading is a type of breakout entry in the direction of the trend. It is a dynamic entry because the breakout entry price level is progressively moved to better prices if the trade is not triggered during the given time period. In the case of potential buy trades, "progressively better prices" refers to progressively *lower* prices. In the case of potential sell (short) trades, "progressively better prices" refers to progressively *higher* prices.

To implement a trailing entry stop in an uptrend, for example, the trader who has just identified the buy signals on the two longer time frames would plan on looking to the shortest time frame to enter the market on a breakout above the previous bar's high. If the current bar closes without breaking the previous bar's high, the breakout level for the next bar would effectively be lowered to the current bar's high. If, in turn, the next bar also does not violate the new breakout level, yet another even lower breakout level is set for the following bar. This process is reversed for potential short trades.

The process of setting the entry level at progressively better prices allows the trader to stay out of trades where the price momentum is not optimal. Resetting of the entry breakout level continues until a breakout in the direction of the trend occurs or the trade setup simply becomes invalid. This latter condition can occur if the original signals on the two longer time frames no longer apply.

During the course of considering a trade using this multiple time frame approach, there are many opportunities for the trader to filter out and abandon the trade if the conditions on the three time frames are not right. But when a position is actually taken using this methodology, it represents a high-probability opportunity that potentially has a greater chance of becoming a successful trade.

Range Trading

Somewhat on the opposite end of the spectrum from trend trading, range trading is the general term for exploiting the ups and downs in

EXHIBIT 14.14

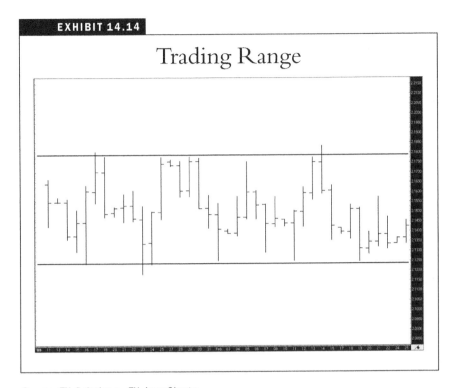

Trading Range

Source: FX Solutions—FX AccuCharts

a sideways, ranging market, as shown in Exhibit 14.14. All financial markets tend often to trade in defined ranges. These ranges can either be clearly defined by horizontal support and resistance boundaries or more ambiguous in their upper and lower borders. Either way, when directional indecision reigns in any particular financial market, a range trading strategy is often the approach of choice.

Integral to the use of any range trading strategy is the identification of market conditions, whether trending or ranging. Techniques for identifying the presence of a trend are the same for identifying a range, or a lack of trend. These include the assessment of moving average slopes (as flat as possible) as well as the rough slopes of volatility bands like the popular Bollinger Bands. Additionally, being able to draw rough resistance and support levels above and below a period of price action is a reliable indicator of the presence of a trading range.

Not every price range is suitable for range trading. Narrow (or short) ranges are generally better suited for breakout trading above resistance or below support. Wide (or tall) ranges are much better suited for range trading, as the expected profit potential between the support and resistance boundaries is greater and therefore more worthwhile from a risk:reward perspective.

When range trading, it is imperative to pay close attention to the management of risk, as profit targets are necessarily limited in magnitude, even with wide ranges. If one is trading long from support at the bottom of a range, the obvious target is the approximate top of the range. Similarly, if one is trading short at resistance near the top of a range, the obvious target is the approximate bottom of the range. Since the expected profit of these range trades is limited by the height of the range itself, unlike the potentially large expected profits of a trend trade, risk management should be kept even tighter and stricter than with other types of trades.

As with other types of technical trades, stop-losses for range trades have a relatively straightforward price location. When entering long at the bottom of a range, a prudent stop-loss may generally be placed directly under the support low of the range. When entering short at the top of a range, a prudent stop-loss may generally be placed directly above the resistance high of the range. These stop-loss areas are locations where the market is telling range traders that they are wrong, as price may be preparing to break out of the trading range.

There are many different methods and strategies for range trading financial markets. With such key technical tools as horizontal support and resistance lines, Bollinger Bands, moving averages, oscillators, and more, the variety of range trading strategies is substantial.

Many technical traders use common horizontal lines on their charts to denote the support and resistance levels in a trading range. At least two touches each, but preferably more, on both the horizontal support and resistance lines are needed in order to establish a trading range with any degree of confidence. Another tool that is commonly used to denote these levels are dynamic volatility bands, most notably the Bollinger Bands. Bollinger Bands have the flexibility to be useful in ranges that do not have the strictly defined upper and lower bounds that are necessary when using horizontal support/resistance lines. If using the Bollinger Bands, range traders have the ability to monitor the slope of the simple moving average running through the middle of the bands to ensure that it is flat, or at least approaching flat. In this way, the traders can have some confirmation that a range trading situation is potentially in place.

On the establishment of a range trading situation using any preferred method, the next step would be to search for potential range trading opportunities. One method involves the use of a common oscillator, such as stochastics or RSI, to confirm turns at or near support and resistance. The customary method of reading these oscillators during ranging markets is straightforward. For potential long trades at or near range support, the oscillator event to watch for would be a cross of the oscillator line(s) above the oversold boundary.

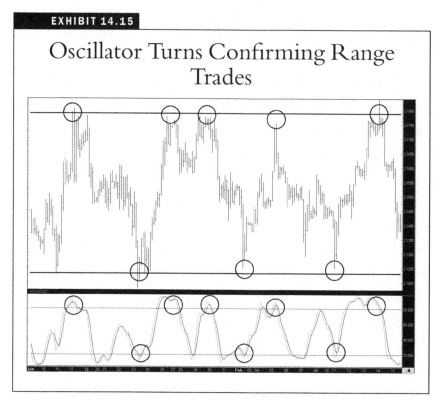

EXHIBIT 14.15

Oscillator Turns Confirming Range Trades

Source: FX Solutions—FX AccuCharts

For potential short trades at or near range resistance, the oscillator event to watch for would be a cross of the oscillator line(s) below the overbought boundary. This is illustrated in Exhibit 14.15.

Another range trade confirmation can be found in trend line breakouts within a range, as shown in Exhibit 14.16. This strategy is a combination of range trading and trend line breakout trading. Within ranges, as price traverses between support and resistance, angled uptrend lines and downtrend lines often form. Breaks of these trend lines can be used as triggers for entering into range trades. Although requiring a trend line break confirmation in this manner

EXHIBIT 14.16

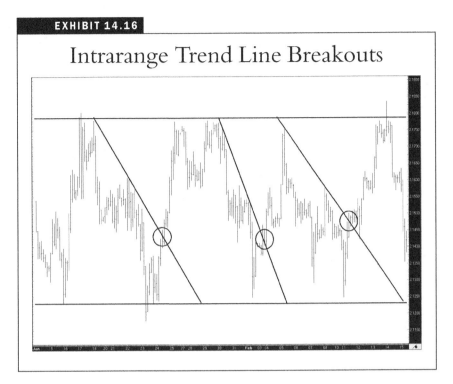

Intrarange Trend Line Breakouts

Source: FX Solutions—FX AccuCharts

almost always leads to a relatively late range trade entry, it generally raises the probability of the trade. This is due to the fact that intrarange trend line breaks represent relatively strong confirmation that a reversal within a range has indeed taken place. With this type of a trade, a tight stop-loss can then be placed on the other side of the broken trend line as opposed to the other side of the range support or resistance. This potentially improves the risk profile for these types of range trades.

Automating range trading strategies can certainly be accomplished for less discretionary methodologies using, for example, such mathematically derived chart elements as Bollinger Bands and oscillator turns. When utilizing support/resistance bounces or intra-range trend line breaks, however, these discretionary components will generally preclude automation.

Like trend trading and breakout trading, range trading can be an effective way of adapting one's trading strategy to ever-changing market conditions. During those market conditions with relatively wide trading ranges, employing strategies that fall under the umbrella of range trading can often be the highest-probability approach.

Price-Oscillator Divergences

Price-oscillator divergences are not generally considered complete strategies unto themselves but instead are usually implemented as an important component of an overall technical trading approach. The most common type of divergence, regular divergence, serves as an early signal that a loss of momentum and a potential reversal may be in the making.

Some traders consider divergences to be exceptionally important signals that should be taken extremely seriously. Other traders are not as convinced. Either way, before any trader should take action on a divergence signal, the signal should be confirmed by other technical factors. In other words, divergences generally should not stand alone as the sole reason to get into any particular trade, as their reliability and usefulness are much greater when used in conjunction with other technical trading elements.

Divergences occur when price and an oscillator diverge in direction. This oscillator can be any of those described in Chapter 10.

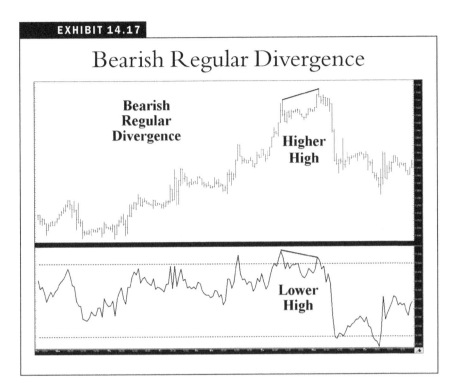

EXHIBIT 14.17

Bearish Regular Divergence

Bearish Regular Divergence

Higher High

Lower High

Source: FX Solutions—FX AccuCharts

Popular possibilities include the RSI, stochastics, ROC, CCI, moving average convergence/divergence (MACD), and Williams %R. But any oscillator can show divergence against price.

As shown in Exhibits 14.17 and 14.18, the primary, and most common, occurrence is called regular divergence. There are two basic manifestations of regular divergence. They are:

1. **Bearish regular divergence.** Price makes a higher high while the oscillator makes a lower high

2. **Bullish regular divergence.** Price makes a lower low while the oscillator makes a higher low

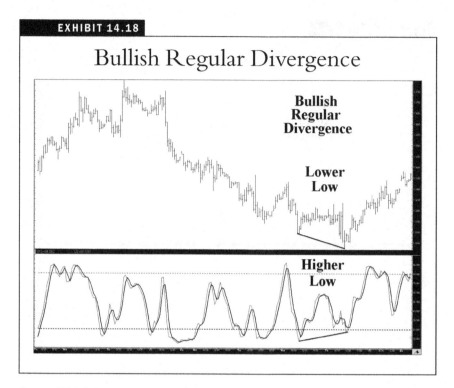

EXHIBIT 14.18

Bullish Regular Divergence

Bullish Regular Divergence

Lower Low

Higher Low

Source: FX Solutions—FX AccuCharts

In both cases, the oscillator shows that the existing momentum that is evident in price action is potentially on the wane. This, in turn, is a tentative indication of a possible impending reversal or perhaps a consolidation.

When regular divergence appears on a chart, it is often recognized immediately by analysts and strategists. These clear-cut signals should not be ignored, as they can often presage a significant price reversal.

Whereas regular divergence is considered a warning of a potential reversal, hidden divergence is just the opposite. A hidden price-oscillator divergence, as shown in Exhibits 14.19 and 14.20, is considered

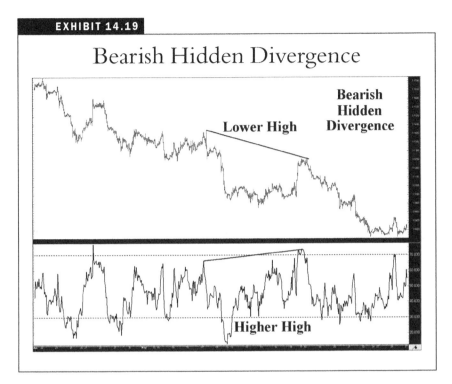

EXHIBIT 14.19

Bearish Hidden Divergence

Source: FX Solutions—FX AccuCharts

a warning of a potential trend continuation. As with regular divergence, there are also two basic manifestations of hidden divergence. They are:

1. **Bearish hidden divergence.** Price makes a lower high while the oscillator makes a higher high

2. **Bullish hidden divergence.** Price makes a higher low while the oscillator makes a lower low

In a bearish hidden divergence, price is in a downtrend. The fact that the oscillator diverges from that downtrend hints at a

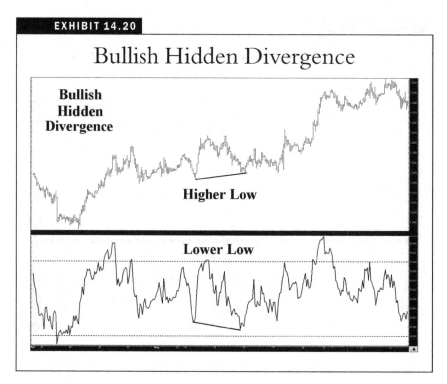

EXHIBIT 14.20

Bullish Hidden Divergence

Bullish Hidden Divergence

Higher Low

Lower Low

Source: FX Solutions—FX AccuCharts

continuation of the downtrend. Conversely, in a bullish hidden divergence, price is in an uptrend. The fact that the oscillator diverges from that uptrend hints at a continuation of the uptrend.

Some traders believe that hidden divergence is a higher-probability trading setup than regular divergence, as hidden divergence is a trend indicator as opposed to a reversal indicator. Trading with the prevailing trend is generally considered by many traders to be of a higher probability.

The search for both types of divergences, regular and hidden, can be automated with the use of alerts on some charting software platforms. However, since divergence trading is not generally a self-contained trading strategy to be used in isolation, it is not generally recommended to automate trading based on incidences of divergence alone.

Oscillator Trading

Aside from their use in identifying divergences, often many oscillators are utilized as the central element of a trading strategy (as opposed to price itself). This may seem unorthodox to many traditional analysts, as price has always been upheld by the vast majority of technical analysts and traders as the single most important aspect of market analysis. Oscillators, after all, are generally just mathematical derivatives of market price. Why would one focus on these by-products of price when one might just as conveniently focus on price itself? The answer to this question lies in the fact that some technical traders have found significant success in concentrating on the movements of certain oscillators, even to the exclusion of the price bars.

Many of the drawings that can be made on price bars can also be made on oscillators. This includes trend lines and horizontal support and resistance lines, as well as some chart patterns. Some traders will take a common oscillator like the RSI or stochastics and draw uptrend lines connecting higher lows, downtrend lines connecting lower highs, or horizontal levels where the oscillator turned and reversed in the past. These lines would then be monitored either for bounces (respect) or breaks (violation). For example, if an uptrend support line is connecting higher lows on the RSI, a breakdown below the trend line indicates a potential reversal in the previous uptrend, much like a breakdown below an uptrend line on price indicates a potential reversal. This could be an indication to trade short in the direction of the potential reversal. For another example, suppose the stochastics oscillator repeatedly visits and turns up at the 40 level. When a bounce up off this 40 level support occurs again, it could be a good potential indication to trade long. Breaks and bounces off trend lines and horizontal support/resistance are traded in much the same way as those on price itself.

Although not technically oscillators, the Bollinger BandWidth indicator and the average true range (ATR) indicator are two volatility analysis tools that look and behave much like oscillators on financial charts. As with oscillators, drawing trend lines and horizontal support/resistance lines can illuminate volatility breakout opportunities on these indicators.

In the example of the Bollinger BandWidth indicator, this is simply a measure of the width between the two Bollinger Bands. BandWidth usually resides in a chart pane above or below the price bars, much as an oscillator normally would. It consists of a single wavy line that denotes the width between the Bollinger Bands. When seeking to trade volatility breakouts on Bollinger Bands, one generally seeks to identify opportunities where low volatility increases dramatically to high volatility. This is also the concept behind the Bollinger Bands squeeze (as discussed earlier in this chapter). On the Bollinger BandWidth indicator, this low-to-high volatility move is manifested by a movement from low to high on the indicator. It can be clarified by using breakouts either of a horizontal resistance line (where BandWidth reached up and turned back down in the past) or a downtrend resistance line (where BandWidth made progressively lower highs in volatility). Breakouts above either of these resistance lines, static or dynamic, can be considered potential areas to jump on a move from low volatility to high volatility. The BandWidth indicator, of course, is not directional in terms of price. It only talks about volatility changes. Therefore, an upside breakout on the Bollinger BandWidth indicator is not necessarily a bullish indication but rather an indication that volatility has increased substantially.

Like the Bollinger BandWidth indicator, the ATR indicator is not an oscillator and is not directional in terms of price. As discussed in Chapter 10, ATR measures periodic price ranges and changes in volatility. It is calculated as a moving average of a given span of past period ranges. Like the BandWidth indicator, ATR consists of a single wavy line that usually resides in a chart pane above or below the price bars. Sharp moves up can be considered significant potential opportunities to participate in low-to-high volatility changes, or volatility breakouts. Therefore, the same practice of drawing a horizontal resistance line (where ATR reached up and turned back down in the past) or a downtrend resistance line (where ATR made progressively lower highs in volatility) can be utilized for identifying upside resistance breakouts, where potential volatility breakout trades can be made. Much as with the Bollinger BandWidth indicator, an upside resistance breakout on the nondirectional ATR is not necessarily a bullish indication but rather an indication that volatility has increased substantially.

TIPS AND TECHNIQUES

Woodie's CCI, Zero–Line Reject

A prominent trader, educator, and CCI specialist by the name of Ken "Woodie" Wood originated a strategy called the zero-line reject, among other CCI-based strategies. Woodie has become well-known among technical traders for having mastered trading with CCI and for sharing his knowledge freely with traders via his Internet forum. Woodie is also known for trading based on CCI moves alone to the exclusion of price; he routinely trades the CCI without even looking at the corresponding price moves. This is a radical departure for most traders, who tend to stress that following price action is the key to technical trading. But Woodie has developed some effective techniques and a large following using CCI alone.

This description does not provide an exhaustive treatment of CCI strategy based on Woodie's method, as several CCI indicator add-ons that he developed are usually used to enhance the basic concept, but the general idea for the zero-line reject strategy is presented here.

A zero-line reject is when the CCI makes a countertrend move to the region around the zero line, which is the middle of the oscillator's range, and then abruptly turns (or gets rejected) and goes back in the direction of the trend. In a trending situation, this simply indicates that price has made a countertrend retracement and then has turned back to continue in the direction of the trend. A CCI zero-line reject trader would get into the trade very shortly after a zero-line area bounce, which means the trader would enter shortly after the countertrend retracement, or pullback, within the trend. This is a high-probability location to get into a trend-following trade. In an uptrend, a CCI zero-line reject would dip down to the zero line from above. In a downtrend, a CCI zero-line reject would rally up to the zero line from below.

Several other oscillators are also routinely used as key components of trading strategies. One of these is the MACD histogram. Like most techniques that involve the use of MACD, this method should be used only when a clear trend has been determined to be in place. The MACD histogram is a key component of the MACD indicator/oscillator and consists of a series of vertical bars that reside in a chart pane above or below the price bars. The histogram oscillates around a zero line and describes the difference between the MACD line and the trigger line. When the histogram's vertical bars cross above the zero line from below and continue rising above it, this is generally a strong indication of bullish price momentum. When the bars cross below the zero line from above and continue falling below it, this is generally a strong indication of bearish price momentum. For this simple MACD histogram trend-following strategy, an entry signal would be given when a histogram bar moves in the direction of the prevailing trend after at least three histogram bars that moved in a countertrend direction. So in an established uptrend, for example, a signal to enter a long trade would be given when a histogram bar is higher than the last histogram bar, but only if at least three directly preceding bars are each lower than the bar preceding it. Much like the CCI zero-line reject method, this MACD histogram entry simply represents a way to get into a trend trade on a significant pullback in the trend, after price has indicated that it is once again ready to go in the direction of the trend. This basic concept of entering trend trades on minor dips in uptrends and minor rallies in downtrends is a recurring theme, both when trading price action directly and when trading an oscillator.

Fibonacci Trading

Much like the traditional role of oscillators and their divergences, Fibonacci analysis is often used to complement other technical trading methods. Some traders, however, consider and use Fibonacci theory as a complete, self-contained trading strategy. As discussed in Chapter 11, Fibonacci theory within financial markets is concerned primarily with percentage retracements, as shown in Exhibit 14.21. Beyond these retracements, however, are also extensions that project price targets. With these rather clear-cut entries and exits, most often

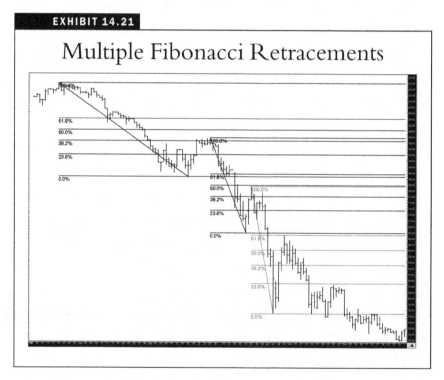

EXHIBIT 14.21

Multiple Fibonacci Retracements

Source: FX Solutions—FX AccuCharts

in the direction of the larger trend, Fibonacci trading is able to stand alone as a relatively complete method of trading.

The primary purpose of Fibonacci analysis is to determine potential retracements within trends. Trends move in one general direction, up or down, but there are always periods of retracement within trends, where price moves in a countertrend manner. In an uptrend, for example, there are invariably a significant number of bearish moves that retrace a portion of the prior bullish moves.

Therefore, there are always minor dips in uptrends and minor rallies in downtrends. These areas are among the most advantageous locations to enter trades in the direction of the trend. In an uptrend, for example, traders always seek to buy low and sell high. Buying on a minor dip within an uptrend means entering at a relatively low price. In a downtrend, traders always seek to sell, or short, high and then buy back, or cover, low. Selling on a minor rally within a downtrend means entering at a relatively high price. These are considered advantageous trade entries.

Fibonacci retracements allow traders to estimate price regions where price may retrace to during dips and rallies. As discussed in Chapter 11, the primary Fibonacci retracement percentages are based on the inverse of the 1.618 Golden Ratio, which is 0.618, or 61.8 percent. Besides this key level, there is also the important 38.2 percent. Another very significant Fibonacci retracement percentage is 50 percent. Other percentages include 23.6 percent and 76.4 percent. For the most part, however, the most popular Fibonacci retracement levels, by far, are 38.2 percent, 50 percent, and 61.8 percent.

Fibonacci retracement percentages are used primarily by traders to forecast the location of potential bounces on dips and rallies where high-probability trade entries may be made. For example, in an uptrend, when a bearish retracement occurs, many traders will wait for any potential bounce around the 38.2 percent retracement of the original uptrend move. If this occurs, these traders may enter long trades, pushing price farther up in its bounce from the 38.2 percent price level.

Another very popular use of Fibonacci analysis includes identifying price targets in the form of extensions. Extensions are Fibonacci percentages above 100 percent that can be used as levels for projecting trade targets. The most popular extension levels watched by traders are at 161.8 percent and 261.8 percent. Other important Fibonacci extension levels include 138.2 percent, 150 percent, and 423.6 percent.

Additionally, Fibonacci levels can be excellent tools for confirming other technical studies, such as traditionally derived support and resistance levels (where price turned or reversed in the past). Fibonacci analysis is one of the most popular aspects of technical analysis in the financial markets. Perhaps because of this, the self-fulfilling prophecy, it is relatively common that significant price action events occur around key Fibonacci price levels.

Positive Expectancy

It is fitting to mention the concept of positive expectancy within a discussion of technical trading strategies. Positive expectancy is the goal of every trader when formulating a trading strategy, as it is one of the absolutely essential keys to achieving consistent profitability. It follows that without a positive expectancy, consistent profitability should not be expected.

If a trading strategy has a positive expectancy, it simply means that the strategy has consistently produced a net gain in equity in the past (as opposed to a net loss). This could mean either a higher average number of winning trades than losses or a greater average profit per winning trade than average loss per losing trade, or some combination of the two.

In order to test and potentially improve a strategy's expectancy, the most common method is to back-test the strategy. Back-testing can take one of two forms: automated or manual. Automated back-testing is reserved for strategies that can be traded on an automated basis, as discussed in the beginning of this chapter. It employs software to apply and record trades according to specific, nondiscretionary rules on historical market price data. Profit/loss results, along with other details of the back-test, are quickly delivered to the back-tester by the software, and the trader can then tweak the parameters of the strategy to fine-tune it for a higher expectancy. If there is a negative expectancy (a net loss on the back-test), the trader can either discard the strategy or alter it substantially and retest.

Manual back-testing may be performed if one wishes to test a discretionary trading strategy that cannot be traded on an automated basis. It consists of looking back manually on historical price charts and applying hypothetical trades by hand according to the strategy's rules. These hypothetical trades should then be observed and recorded to obtain a long-term record of performance. This is a long and labor-intensive process but is well worth the effort if one wishes to test and improve a manually traded strategy.

Besides back-testing, yet another method for testing and improving the expectancy of a strategy is to forward-test it. This consists of actually trading the strategy in real time, preferably with a demo or practice trading account, and recording the performance results. Although this is probably the most effective and accurate way to test a strategy, it has a substantial limitation in its slowness of obtaining results.

Whichever method is used to test and tweak expectancy, it cannot be emphasized enough that the work of testing absolutely needs to be performed in order to have a chance at attaining consistent profitability in trading.

Summary

This chapter provided descriptions of common technical trading strategies. These strategies comprise the practical application of all the essential technical analysis knowledge covered in this book thus far. Some of the strategies described can be traded in an automated fashion, while others can only be traded manually. This is primarily contingent on whether the strategy has a subjective, discretionary component, in which case it would need to be traded on a manual basis.

Beginning with several varieties of moving average crossovers, the strategy descriptions then moved onto the popular methodologies of breakout trading, trend trading, range trading, divergence trading, oscillator trading, and Fibonacci trading. These different methods fit different markets, types of traders, and styles of trading. Each can be tailored specifically according to an individual trader's own testing and experimentation. The chapter concluded with a discussion of the importance of achieving positive expectancy when formulating trading strategies. Expectancy can be tested and improved on through the use of back-testing, both manual and automated, as well as forward-testing.

CHAPTER 15

Risk Control and Money Management

After reading this chapter, you will be able to:

- Realize that risk control and money management are among the most important aspects of successful trading.

- Appreciate that knowledge of technical analysis can contribute substantially to implementing a solid risk management strategy.

- Understand the key roles that stop-losses, risk:reward ratios, position sizing, maximum loss percentage, multiple fractional positions, and diversification play in avoiding catastrophe and pursuing consistent net profitability as a technical trader.

Introduction to Risk Control and Money Management

No discussion of technical analysis would be complete without mention of risk control and money management as they relate to technical analysis. Many beginning traders in all the major financial markets become almost immediately enamored with trade entries. They are in constant search for that holy grail of trading strategies that will get them into winning trades on a consistent basis.

What many traders, especially beginners, lack is an adequate grounding in the proper approach to risk and money management. Without these key components of successful trading, failure is almost assured. Conversely, if good risk and money management are securely in place, even traders with less than stellar trade entry strategies can survive and even thrive.

Many people who have even limited exposure to financial markets are aware that technical analysis excels at providing concrete trade entry locations. For example, an entry on a head-and-shoulders reversal would generally be on or shortly after a breakdown of the neckline. Similarly, an entry within a moving average crossover strategy would be on or shortly after a cross of the shorter-period moving average over the longer-period moving average. Whenever a technical study is involved in making a trade, chances are that there is a well-defined entry specified.

While many know that technical analysis provides these straightforward entries, some are unaware that trade exits, whether in loss or in profit, are just as strong and well defined as entries.

262

Furthermore, these exits are the basis for an intelligent and prudent approach to proper risk management.

Stop-Losses

With regard to exits, technical analysis excels at facilitating initial stop-loss placement as well as dynamic stop-loss placement once a given trade has entered into profit. In addition, technical analysis also supplies potential profit target exits.

In setting initial stop-losses, the underlying philosophy as dictated by technical analysis principles is to get out of any trade once the market proves that your original reason for getting into the trade was wrong, an example of which is illustrated in Exhibit 15.1. For example, if a long trade is entered shortly after the breakout of a major resistance level, there are several logical locations for an initial stop-loss. For one, a stop-loss can be placed right below the resistance level, as a price reversion back below that level will have proven that the original reason for getting into the trade (a breakout) was ultimately wrong, at least for the time being. Perhaps more practically, however, the stop-loss might be better placed right below the closest swing low that resides below the resistance level. This is due to the frequent tendency of breakout moves to fluctuate around support or resistance before either making a true breakout or failing altogether.

The concept of getting out when the basis for a trade is wrong can also be extended to dynamic stop-losses, otherwise known as trailing stops. The technique of trailing stops allows traders to lock

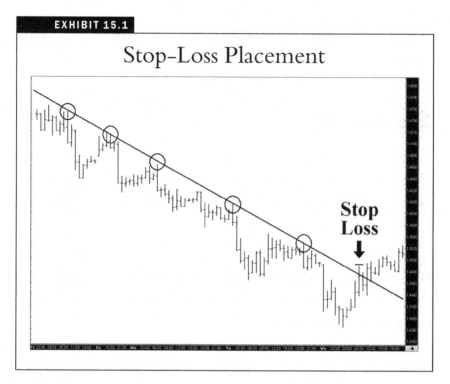

EXHIBIT 15.1

Stop-Loss Placement

Source: FX Solutions—FX AccuCharts

in profits while progressively limiting risk during the course of a trade that moves into greater profit. The type of trailing stop discussed here is the manual variety, as opposed to the automated variety. Manual trailing stop-losses depend on the trader to move the stop-loss manually, in the direction of profit, when the opportunity presents itself. In an uptrend situation, for example, when a long trade is already in profit, the trader would move the stop-loss progressively higher as price continues to move in the direction of the trade. The location for each of these stop-loss moves mirrors initial stop-loss placement very closely. As price recovers from each minor dip, or swing low, in the uptrend, the trader would move the trailing stop-loss to just under the last swing low. If price breaks down below the last swing low, it is a strong indication that the trend might be changing or reversing. In this instance, the trend-following trade should be terminated, as the reason for staying in the trade, which is the prevailing uptrend, will have been seriously challenged with a breakdown below the last swing low. Conversely, if price continues to make progressively higher swing lows, the trailing stop may continue to be trailed, locking in progressively greater profits.

Trade exits are an important aspect of risk control using technical analysis. Risk control has two primary purposes. One purpose is never to have a single catastrophic loss cripple one's trading account. When stop-losses are measured and predetermined according to strict rules of risk control and money management, one can be assured that any single loss, and even any moderate string of losses, can be absorbed without too much pain. The second purpose of proper risk control is that it helps foster an environment where overall profit can exceed overall loss, preferably by a substantial amount. Clearly, this principle is absolutely crucial to achieving consistent profitability as a trader.

It follows that the single most important priority for all successful traders is the preservation of capital. Risk and money must be managed in a manner such that the ultimate goal is to survive to trade another day. Without a firm grounding in this principle, an undisciplined trader is doomed from the outset. Many experienced traders go a step further by subscribing to the winning philosophy that if virtually every ounce of focus is concentrated on preserving capital, the profits will take care of themselves.

Reward:Risk Ratio

One of the key components to a good risk management plan that is closely related to the preservation of capital is an optimal risk:reward ratio. This ratio can be fine-tuned using predetermined stop-losses and profit targets that are derived from the prudent use of technical analysis concepts. As mentioned earlier in this chapter, technical analysis provides precise price locations for initial stop-losses, dynamic stop-losses, and profit targets. Knowing how to set these elements of a trade is sufficient for establishing and working within the guidelines of an optimal risk:reward ratio.

First, it should be established that when one hears about a 3:1 ratio or a 4:1 ratio, what is generally being referred to is a reward:risk ratio rather than the reverse. Therefore, this section adopts this reward:risk naming convention.

The reward:risk ratio is a simple concept that can contribute a great deal to any trader's net profitability. While optimal reward:risk ratios can be difficult to attain in everyday trading, all traders should always strive to attain the highest ratios that are practically possible.

To provide an illustration of reward to risk, suppose a trader targets a 3:1 ratio. This simply means that on any given trade, the trader is seeking to profit by at least three times the amount that he or she is prepared to lose. In real-world terms, this means that if a trade is entered with a $1000 stop-loss, for example, the profit target would need to be set to at least $3000. This would be a $3000:$1000, or a 3:1 reward:risk ratio.

The ramifications of the reward:risk ratio are considerable. With a high ratio, traders can actually lose significantly more trades than they win and still be consistently profitable. This is because their average profits are much larger than their average losses. The concept of a high reward:risk ratio lends itself well to the oft-repeated traders' maxim, "Let your profits run and cut your losses short."

Technical analysis lends itself well to setting an optimal reward: risk ratio in one's trading. As mentioned earlier, stop-loss placement is straightforward when trading technically. Trades should be terminated as soon as the market has proven that the original reason for getting into the trade was wrong. This usually means that stop-losses should be placed beyond certain lines or price levels. Since the loss aspect of the reward:risk ratio is straightforward, it requires only a calculation of the profit aspect in order to decide whether a particular trade conforms to one's minimum ratio and therefore if that particular trade is indeed worth taking.

Profit targets are not as straightforward to set as stop-losses. When it comes down to it, no one can ever know definitively where or how far price will go. That is why trailing stop-losses are popular trading tools—they allow traders to lock in profits while still letting profits run, even if the ultimate price destination is utterly unknown.

For the purposes of keeping to a reasonable and profitable reward:risk ratio, however, concrete profit targets need to be used. As mentioned in several places throughout this book, there are built-in profit targets for most types of technical trades. Chart pattern trades (e.g., head and shoulders, triangles, rectangles, flags, pennants, etc.), for example, have clear built-in targets. Similarly, both parallel trend channels and horizontal trading ranges have targets at the far side of the channel or range. Support/resistance breakout trades have targets of further support or resistance levels. Fibonacci extensions can also be used to determine trade targets. Once a realistic profit target for a particular trade is identified, a decision can be made as to whether the trade fits the reward:risk ratio criteria set by the trader prior to the trade. For example, if the trader has set a minimum reward:risk ratio of 2:1, and the stop-loss is set at a $3000 loss, the profit target must represent a minimum of $6000 in profit.

There are many instances where a reward:risk ratio requirement would preclude entering into a particular trade by a prudent trader or investor. One example often occurs at support or resistance break-outs. Assuming a breakout trader waits for the close of the breakout bar before entering a trade, if the price bar that breaks out above a certain resistance level or below a certain support level is an extremely long bar (i.e., the bar that breaks out represents an inordi-nately substantial price move), the reward:risk ratio may be skewed, and the trader may wisely decide to stay out of the trade. This is because if the breakout bar is too long, the stop-loss, which is cus-tomarily placed on the other side of the break, would necessarily be located at a greater distance than if the breakout bar was smaller. A greater distance means that the potential monetary loss is greater. In turn, this means that a substantially larger profit target must be identi-fied in order to make the trade worthwhile from a reward:risk perspective.

What exactly is the optimal reward:risk ratio? It really depends on the trading strategy used and the trader's particular style of trading. In practical day-to-day trading, it can be difficult to attain ratios as high as 4:1, because with higher ratios, the clear trade-off is that losses be-come much more frequent than wins. Since the wins would be much larger in dollar value than the losses, this is acceptable from a long-term profitability standpoint. But the psychological toll of excessively frequent losses, even if relatively smaller in value, can eventually become devastating for a trader who does not possess a steel will and iron determination. Practically speaking, depending on one's trading strategy and style of trading, many traders seek to target a reward:risk ratio of at least 2:1 or 3:1. This means that each trade profit is targeted to be at least two times or three times as large as each loss. Of course, many traders have lower reward:risk ratios, but their expected win ratio needs to be proportionately higher in order to compensate and achieve consistent profitability.

Maximum Allowable Loss

Besides targeting an optimal reward:risk ratio, traders should also set a maximum allowable loss per trade. This is often called fixed fractional money management and refers to a percentage of total account equity. Setting a maximum loss limit is crucial to the all-important goal of preserving capital.

Many traders will set a maximum loss percentage, such as 2 percent, and then set their stop-loss so it corresponds to the dollar value that is represented by that percentage. Technical traders who have the ability to enter flexible trade sizes, however, have a better, less arbitrary way to fix their maximum loss.

As mentioned throughout this book, technical analysis affords an optimal approach to setting stop-losses according to market price action, not according to an arbitrary dollar amount. When setting a maximum loss limit, this approach should be preserved. Therefore, prudent technical traders will first set their stop-losses according to the market (where price action proves the original reasons for getting into the trade to be wrong) and then set the size of the trade position in conjunction with the size of the stop-loss to conform to the maximum loss percentage. Therefore, if the stop-loss represents a greater loss according to market price action, the trade position size should be set to a smaller value in order to conform to the acceptable loss limit. Conversely, if the stop-loss represents a smaller loss according to market price action, the trade position size may be set to a greater value to conform to the acceptable loss limit.

To provide a simple example as it relates to the spot foreign exchange (forex) market, suppose a maximum loss limit as a percentage of total account equity is set by the trader at 2 percent for each trade. The trader has $50,000 in a forex trading account. Two percent of $50,000 is $1000, so that is the maximum that the trader is willing to lose on any given trade. If a stop-loss is dictated by market price action to be located 20 pips (currency price increments) away from the trade entry, the trade size should be set to a value at which 20 pips equals $1000. This would be five lots (standard currency contracts), as the pip value on this five-lot trade size equals $50 per pip. If, however, a stop-loss is dictated by the market to be located 100 pips away from the trade entry, the trade size should be set to a value at which 100 pips equals $1000. This would be one lot, as the pip value on this one-lot trade size equals $10 per pip.

This approach ensures that one can set stop-losses logically according to technical analysis principles while also allowing for fine-tuning of the percentage loss according to a predetermined maximum loss level.

What is the optimal percentage to set as this maximum loss level? It depends on many factors, including the trading strategy used and the trader's specific risk tolerance. The figure that is most often talked about in trading circles is a maximum loss of 2 percent of account equity per trade. For many traders, this figure is reasonable. However, for many professional traders, 2 percent can be considered high, so some opt for 1 percent or even lower. More aggressive traders may set a higher maximum loss, sometimes well above 2 percent. Capping losses can only be a good thing. Along with proper position sizing based on the equity in one's trading account, limiting risk in this way can help one achieve longevity in trading.

Multiple Fractional Positions

Closely related to prudent position sizing is the practice of entering multiple fractional positions rather than entering a single full position for each trade. This is a solid method to help spread and control risk. Multiple fractional positions are smaller components of a full-size trade. These multiple positions may all be entered at the same time and at a single price level, much like a full-size position, but their exits can be staggered when in profit. Each fractional position can be progressively closed in a staggered manner to lock in profits as price moves in a profitable direction. This method, of course, can be practiced only if the market traded offers flexible position sizes and/or if the trader has enough capital to enter multiple positions for each trade.

For example, instead of buying a single large position of a certain security at a certain price, three fractional positions that each comprise one-third the size of the original single position can all be bought at the same price. Initial stop-losses for all three of these position can be set in the same manner as if they were a single full position. If price moves in the direction of profit for these positions, one of the positions can be closed for a profit at a certain price point (technically determined) while the other two are allowed to run further. At this point, the initial stop-losses for the two remaining positions may be tightened to break even. If price continues to move toward increasing profit, another position may be closed for an even larger profit than the first, again at a technically determined profit level. The previously trailed stop-loss on the third fractional position (now at breakeven) may then be tightened even further to lock in additional profit. Finally, if price continues to move in the direction of profit, the third position may be closed for a final profit at a third technically determined price level, or the stop-loss may continue to be trailed until it is ultimately hit by price action and the position is closed at a non-predetermined profit level.

This multiple position approach combines the best of both worlds—locking in profits while, at the same time, letting profits run. At any point after the first fractional profit is taken, the trader employing this method can be assured that at least some profit is taken off the table, while the remaining positions are protected from loss by the trailed stop-losses. Since no trader can ever be sure how long price will run, this method helps manage profit situations in a prudent and effective manner.

Diversification

Another important way to spread and control risk in trading is by diversifying one's trades/investments. For obvious reasons, this is crucial for limiting one's market risk. Entering positions that are too closely correlated, whether in the same asset class or different asset classes, can be disastrous. This is not quite the equivalent of overloading on a single position in a single market or security, but it can come close. Markets that are correlated, whether positively or negatively, often move together. This can be dangerous if a trader is involved in trading multiple, correlated markets. In these situations, adverse price moves that are correlated in different markets can severely damage an otherwise healthy trading account. For this reason alone, every trader should be extremely wary of all the possible correlations that may exist among the many different markets that can be traded.

Overall, the components of good risk control and money management are absolutely crucial to achieving success in trading and investing. Combined with hands-on experience and a solid understanding of the essentials of technical analysis, prudent risk and money management are the keys to attaining the ultimate goal of trading financial markets: consistent profitability.

Summary

This chapter provided an introduction to the all-important concepts of risk control and money management. More often than not, these two factors make the difference between successful traders and unsuccessful traders. Technical analysis can contribute substantially to implementing a solid risk and money management strategy. Key concepts include stop-losses, risk:reward ratio, position sizing, maximum allowable loss, multiple fractional positioning, and diversification.

The philosophy behind technically determined stop-losses is to automatically get out of any trade once the market proves that one's original reason for getting into the trade was wrong. This is a necessity in order to preserve capital, avoid catastrophic losses, and have overall profits exceed overall losses.

A focus on one's risk:reward ratio, or reward:risk ratio, is a key component of a good trading plan. Optimal ratios can be difficult to achieve, but a minimum threshold should be met in order to have a chance at consistent profitability. Reward:risk ratio is simply the amount of profit on a trade that is targeted in comparison with the amount of loss that is allowed. For example, a ratio of 2:1 on a trade means that the profit target is two times the size of the allowed loss. Higher ratios allow for more frequent trading losses while still providing an opportunity to achieve overall net profitability.

Maximum allowable loss refers to a predetermined maximum percentage of equity that a trader sets to represent an acceptable amount of loss per trade. For example, if this percentage is set at 2 percent, it means that the trader can accept a loss of 2 percent of account equity per trade. Limiting the amount of loss per trade in this way helps preserve capital and avoid catastrophic losses. The methodology used to implement this practice usually centers around setting stop-losses. A technical trader will generally set the stop-loss according to a market-determined location (e.g., beyond a support/resistance level, under a dip, or above a rally) and then adjust position sizing according to how wide the stop-loss ends up being, in conjunction with the trader's predetermined maximum allowable loss.

Multiple fractional positioning is a method of spreading and controlling risk that involves opening multiple smaller positions in place of a single full-size position. This aids in fostering an effective profit-taking process because it allows traders simultaneously to lock in profits while letting profits run.

Diversification is also a key element of spreading and controlling risk. Getting involved simultaneously in closely correlated markets can become a disaster if and when adverse price moves occur. Therefore, prudent traders should always make sure that the markets they commit to at any given time are not too closely correlated, whether positively or negatively.

Index

A

Appel, Gerald, 21, 140
Automated trading, 23–24, 202, 222
Average directional index (ADX) indicator, 21, 142–144, 209
Average true range (ATR) indicator, 21, 144, 251

B

Back-testing, 257–258
Bar charts, 34–36
Basso, Tom, 46
Bollinger, John, 22, 140
Bollinger Bands indicator, 22, 140–141, 241
Bollinger Bands squeeze, 141, 222
Bollinger BandWidth indicator, 250–251

Breakouts, support and resistance, 59–64
Breakout trading, 212–223

C

Candlestick charts, 34–37
Candlestick patterns:
   doji, 112–113
   engulfing, 117
   hammer, 113
   hanging man, 115
   harami, 117
   inverted hammer, 115–116
   multiple-candle, 116–118
   overview of, 110–118
   pin bars, 114
   shooting star, 113–114
   single-candle, 111–116
   spinning top, 113
   window, 109

Ceiling, resistance as, 30, 58, 59, 64

Channels. *See* Trend channels

Chartered Market Technician (CMT), 23

Chart patterns. *See* Patterns, chart

Charts, history of, 17–18

Commodity channel index (CCI) oscillator, 21, 157–159, 252

Confirmation, trend. *See* Trend confirmation

Confluence, 209–211

Continuation patterns. *See* Patterns, continuation

Corrective waves, *see* Elliott Wave

Covel, Michael, 45–50

Crossovers, moving average. *See* Moving averages, crossovers

D

Dennis, Richard, 22, 223

Divergences, 148–151, 197–198, 244–249

Diversification, 273

Donchian, Richard, 22

Double bottom. *See* Patterns, double bottom

Double top. *See* Patterns, double top

Dow, Charles, 14, 17

Dow theory, 14–17

Downtrends, 43

E

Edwards, Robert, 20–21

Elder, Dr. Alexander, 232–234

Elliott, Ralph Nelson, 18–19, 170

Elliott Wave:
  alternation, 174
  channels, 173
  corrective waves, 171–172
  guidelines, 173
  motive waves, 170–171
  structure, 170–173
  theory, 18–19, 44–45, 170–175

Emotions, impact on market, 28–29, 58

Entry filters, 80, 87, 208–209, 219
  bounce bars, 227

countertrend breakouts,
    228–229
  pullbacks, 220–221
  throwbacks, 220–221
Expectancy, positive, 256–258

F
Fibonacci:
  arc, 167–168
  extensions, 165–166, 256
  fan, 166–167
  Golden Ratio, 162, 163, 166,
    255
  and Leonardo, 162
  Liber Abaci, 162
  retracements, 162–165,
    255–256
  sequence, 162
  theory, 161–170
  time zones, 168–169
  trading, 254–256
Fixed fractional money
    management, 269–271
Flag. *See* Patterns, flag
Floor, support as, 30, 59, 64
Foreign exchange markets, 3,
    107, 194, 199, 270
Forward-testing, 258

Fractional positions, 271–272
Fundamental analysis, 2–3, 47
Futures markets, 2–3, 22, 194,

G
Gann, W. D., 20
Gaps:
  breakaway, 107–108
  common, 107
  concept of, 106–109
  exhaustion, 108
  island reversal, 108–109
  runaway, 108
Granville, Joseph, 197
*Granville's New Key to Stock
    Market Profits*, 197

H
Head-and-shoulders. *See*
    Patterns, head-and-
    shoulders
Honma, Munehisa, 12–14

I
Indicators:
  oscillators, *see* Oscillators
  overview, 20–22, 25, 135–159
  universal, 136

J

Japanese rice markets, 12–14, 36

L

Lambert, Donald, 21, 157

Lane, George, 21, 154

Linear regression indicator,
  146–147

Line charts, 37–38

M

Magee, John, 20–21

Market Technicians Association
  (MTA), 19, 23

Maximum allowable loss,
  269–271

Motive waves, *see* Elliott Wave

Moving average convergence/
  divergence (MACD):
  histogram, 253
  overview of, 21, 139–140

Moving averages:
  concept of, 119–123
  correct order of, 128–130, 236
  crossovers, 123–131, 203–209
  exponential (EMA), 121–122
  lag, 130–131
  look-back period, 121

multiple, 128–130

simple (SMA), 121–122

support and resistance,
  131–133

trend trading, 230–232

weighted (WMA), 121–122

whipsaws, 127–128, 207–208

Multiple fractional positions,
  271–272

Multiple time frame trading,
  234–238

N

New Concepts in Technical
  Trading Systems, 21, 151

Nison, Steve, 12–13, 18, 36, 110

O

OHLC (Open, High, Low,
  Close), 34, 35, 40, 190

On-balance volume (OBV),
  196–198

Oscillators, 138–139, 148–159,
  249–253
  commodity channel index
    (CCI), 157–159
  and divergence, 148–151,
    234–239

rate of change (ROC),
     156–157
relative strength index (RSI),
     151–154,
     stochastics, 154–156
Osaka, Japan, 13, 24

P
Parabolic stop and reverse (SAR)
     indicator, 21, 144–146
Parallel trend channels. *See*
     Trend channels
Paralysis by analysis, 136–137,
     210
Patterns:
     candlestick, 110–118. *See also*
          Candlestick patterns
     chart, 30, 91–100, 102–118
     continuation, 93–100
     double bottom, 102–103
     double top, 102–103
     flag, 96–97
     gap, 106–109. *See also* Gaps
     head-and-shoulders, 104–106
     pennant, 96–98
     point-and-figure, 181–188.
          See also Point-and-figure
          charts

rectangle, 98–99
reversal, 102–106
triangle, 93–96
triple bottom, 104
triple top, 104
wedge, 100
Pennant. *See* Patterns, pennant
Perceptions, impact of market,
     28–29
Pivot points, 68–72
Point-and-figure charts:
     box size, 180
     overview, 38–40, 177–181
     patterns, 181–188
     price targets, 188–190
     reversal amount, 180
Position sizing, 270–272
Prechter, Robert Jr., 4–5, 19,
     170
Price action, 28–32
     cycle, 170
Pullbacks and throwbacks,
     220–221

R
Ranges, trading, 60,
     239–240
Range trading, 238–244

Rate of change (ROC) oscillator, 156–157

Rectangle. *See* Patterns,
rectangle

Relative strength index (RSI)
oscillator, 21, 151–154

Reversal patterns. *See* Patterns,
reversal

Risk:reward ratio, 266–269

S

Self-fulfilling prophecy, 31, 164

Seykota, Ed, 49–50

Stochastics oscillator, 21,
154–156

Stop-loss placement, 80–81, 87,
218, 230, 240–241,
263–265

Support and resistance:
concept of, 30, 58–64, 66–89
dynamic, 72–77
lines, horizontal, 78–81, 241
moving averages, 131–133
static, 67–71

T

Technical analysis, description
of, 2–3

Technical Analysis of Stock Trends,
20–21

Tick volume, 198

Time frames, chart, 50–51

Trading strategies, overview of,
202–258

Trend:
channels, 52–54, 74–78,
87–89
concept of, 15–17, 29, 42–45,
50–51, 75
confirmation, 16
lack of, 44
lines, 54–55, 72–74, 81–87,
226–227

Trend following, 22, 223–224

Trend trading, 224–238

Triangle. *See* Patterns, triangle

Triple Screen trading system,
232–234

Triple bottom. *See* Patterns,
triple bottom

Triple top. *See* Patterns, triple
top

"Turtles" trading, 22, 223–224

U

Uptrends, 43

V

Volatility, 100–101

Volume, 16, 193–198

W

Wall Street, 47, 48, 50

Wedge. *See* Patterns, wedge

Wilder, J. Welles, 21, 142, 144,
    145, 151, 209

Williams %R, 149, 160, 236,
    245

Wood, Ken ("Woodie"),
    252

Z

Zero line, 140, 157, 158, 252,
    253

Zero-line reject, 252

Made in the USA
Las Vegas, NV
23 January 2021

16394034R00168